A Taxonomy of Cognitive Semantics

Linguistics

Volumes published in this Brill Research Perspectives title are listed at *brill.com/rplis*

A Taxonomy of Cognitive Semantics

By

Leonard Talmy

BRILL

LEIDEN | BOSTON

Library of Congress Control Number: 2025933473

Typeface for the Latin, Greek, and Cyrillic scripts: "Brill". See and download: brill.com/brill-typeface.

ISSN 2667-0682
ISBN 978-90-04-73025-0 (paperback)
ISBN 978-90-04-73026-7 (e-book)
DOI 10.1163/9789004730267

Copyright 2025 by Leonard Talmy. Published by Koninklijke Brill BV, Plantijnstraat 2, 2321 JC Leiden, The Netherlands.
Koninklijke Brill BV incorporates the imprints Brill, Brill Nijhoff, Brill Schöningh, Brill Fink, Brill mentis, Brill Wageningen Academic, Vandenhoeck & Ruprecht, Böhlau and V&R unipress.
Koninklijke Brill BV reserves the right to protect this publication against unauthorized use. Requests for re-use and/or translations must be addressed to Koninklijke Brill BV via brill.com or copyright.com.
For more information: info@brill.com.

This book is printed on acid-free paper and produced in a sustainable manner.

Contents

Acknowledgments   IX
Introduction   1
1 Major Language Divisions (A)   4
   1.1 *Form (A1)*   4
   1.2 *Grammar (A2)*   4
      1.2.1 Morpheme (A2a)   5
      1.2.2 Closed Class (A2b)   6
      1.2.3 Open Class (A2c)   7
      1.2.4 Morpheme Types within Multimorphemic Words (A2d)   7
      1.2.5 Contrasting Open- and Closed-Class Status (A2e)   8
   1.3 *Meaning (A3)*   8
   1.4 *Context (A4)*   9
2 Participant Structure (B)   10
   2.1 *Participant Type (B1)*   10
   2.2 *Participant Numbers (B2)*   10
   2.3 *Participant Directionality (B3)*   10
3 Arenas of Assembly (C)   10
   3.1 *Inventory (C1)*   11
   3.2 *Expression (C2)*   11
   3.3 *Part Inventory, Part Expression (C3)*   11
4 Content Structuring Mechanisms (D)   12
   4.1 *Closed-Class Semantics (D1)*   12
      4.1.1 Configurational Structure (D1a)   13
      4.1.2 Perspective (D1b)   16
      4.1.3 Attention (D1c)   16
      4.1.4 Force Dynamics (D1d)   17
      4.1.5 Cognitive State (D1e)   18
      4.1.6 Reality Status (D1f)   21
      4.1.7 Communicative Purpose (D1g)   23
      4.1.8 Role Semantics (D1h)   25
      4.1.9 Quantity (D1i)   27
      4.1.10 Ontology (D1j)   28
   4.2 *Content Patterning (D2)*   30
      4.2.1 In the Morpheme (D2a)   30
      4.2.2 In the Lexicon (D2b)   32
      4.2.3 In Expression (D2c)   34

- 4.3 *Content Selection (D3)*   35
  - 4.3.1 Inclusion vs. Omission (D3a)   35
  - 4.3.2 Alternatives of Inclusion (D3b)   38
  - 4.3.3 Constraints on Selection (D3c)   39
- 4.4 *Content Inference (D4)*   40
- 4.5 *Context (D5)*   40
  - 4.5.1 Context for Speaker Omission and Hearer Inference (D5a)   40
  - 4.5.2 Context for Speaker Selection among Alternatives (D5b)   41
  - 4.5.3 Context for Other Hearer Interpretation (D5c)   42
- 4.6 *Interaction (D6)*   43
  - 4.6.1 Cross-Consideration (D6a)   43
  - 4.6.2 Turn Taking (D6b)   44

5 Combination (E)   45
- 5.1 *Additive (E1)*   46
  - 5.1.1 Within a Hierarchy (E1a)   46
  - 5.1.2 Across Language Divisions (E1b)   48
  - 5.1.3 In Contraction/Suppletion (E1c)   49
  - 5.1.4 In Conflation (E1d)   49
  - 5.1.5 In Nesting (E1e)   50
- 5.2 *Operational (E2)*   51
- 5.3 *Idiomatic (E3)*   52
- 5.4 *Constructively Discrepant (E4)*   53
  - 5.4.1 Conflict between Morphemes (E4a)   53
  - 5.4.2 Conflict between Utterance and General Knowledge (E4b)   56

6 Diachronic Comparison (F)   56
- 6.1 *Long Time Scale (F1)*   57
- 6.2 *Medium Time Scale (F2)*   59
- 6.3 *Short Time Scale (F3)*   60

7 Crosslinguistic Comparison (G)   60
- 7.1 *Scope of Comparison (G1)*   60
- 7.2 *Absolutely Universal (G2)*   61
  - 7.2.1 Positive Universals (G2a)   61
  - 7.2.2 Negative Universals (G2b)   62
  - 7.2.3 Explanations of Universality (G2c)   63
- 7.3 *Typological (G3)*   64

- 7.4 *Repertorial (G4)* 65
  - 7.4.1 The Level of Schematic Systems (G4a) 65
  - 7.4.2 The Level of Conceptual Categories within a Schematic System (G4b) 66
  - 7.4.3 The Level of Semantic Components within a Conceptual Category (G4c) 66
- 7.5 *Indefinitely Diverse (G5)* 67
  - 7.5.1 Morphemic Meaning (G5a) 67
  - 7.5.2 Range of Applicability (G5b) 68
  - 7.5.3 Polysemous Range (G5c) 68
  - 7.5.4 Partitioning of a Semantic Area (G5d) 69

8 Quantity of Manifestation (H) 69
- 8.1 *Elaboratedness (H1)* 69
  - 8.1.1 In a Communication System (H1a) 70
  - 8.1.2 In a Language User (H1b) 70
  - 8.1.3 In a Lexicon (H1c) 71
  - 8.1.4 In Expression (H1d) 71
- 8.2 *Prevalence (H2)* 72
  - 8.2.1 Compared across Languages (H2a) 72
  - 8.2.2 In a Single Language (H2b) 73

9 Communication Systems (I) 74
- 9.1 *Co-speech Gesture (I1)* 76
  - 9.1.1 Targeting Gestures (I1a) 76
  - 9.1.2 Nontargeting Gestures (I1b) 77
- 9.2 *Signed Language (I2)* 77
  - 9.2.1 Number of Independent Parameters (I2a) 78
  - 9.2.2 Scene Partitioning (I2b) 78
  - 9.2.3 Iconicity (I2c) 79

10 Relations across Cognitive Faculties (J) 79
- 10.1 *Language's External Relations to Other Cognitive Systems (J1)* 80
  - 10.1.1 Noncommonality of Organization (J1a) 80
  - 10.1.2 Commonality of Organization (J1b) 82
- 10.2 *Language's Internal Relations to Other Cognitive Faculties (J2)* 86
  - 10.2.1 Faculties Underlying Morphemes (J2a) 86
  - 10.2.2 Faculties Underlying Extended Communication (J2b) 87
  - 10.2.3 Faculties Underlying Certain Semantic Distinctions (J2c) 89
  - 10.2.4 Limitations on Faculty Coordination (J2d) 90

11 Research Characteristics (K) 93
  11.1 *Methodology* (*K1*) 93
  11.2 *Other Aspects of Approach* (*K2*) 95
  Conclusion 95
  References 96
  Index 101

Acknowledgments

My great thanks to Thomas Fuyin Li for his unparalleled work in promoting and contributing to cognitive semantics, helping in the expansion of the field that this book reports on. I thank Uri Tadmor at Brill as well for suggesting the publication of this book. And as always, my great thanks to Stacy Krainz for her help with research and editing.

A Taxonomy of Cognitive Semantics

Leonard Talmy
Department of Linguistics, Center for Cognitive Science,
University at Buffalo, State University of New York, USA
talmy@buffalo.edu

Introduction

The central concern of cognitive semantics is how language structures conceptual content. More specifically, it addresses a conceptual range that includes both ideation and affect and concerns how this range is organized into patterns and processes in language. This concern distinguishes it from such other areas of linguistic research as phonology and syntax when undertaken without consideration of meaning.

Cognitive semantics, further, treats the conceptual structuring that it observes in language not as a research end in itself but as a window onto cognitive organization in general, that is, how the mind works. It thus allies with such other approaches as cognitive psychology and forms part of cognitive science. This larger concern is what distinguishes it from traditional semantics.

Since its origins, cognitive semantics has grown greatly in the range and depth of its research on conceptual structure in language. This expansion is represented in the *Handbook for Cognitive Semantics* (Li, 2022), whose forty-five chapters map out the field's current extent. The present book in fact consists of the Foreword to that Handbook (Talmy, 2022) together with a journal article (Talmy, 2023) written as an augment to the Foreword and here appearing as Part 10. Both have here been substantially revised.

This book presents a taxonomy of cognitive semantics. The aim is to approach the field comprehensively and outline its main contours. To do this, it both summarizes previous research and presents novel analyses. But this taxonomy is only heuristic—it is an initial endeavor to survey the field and is meant to be developed. It inevitably has omissions that could be filled and analyses that could be structured otherwise. The intention, though, is to provide a basis for discussion.

The taxonomy is organized in terms of categories and subcategories into which conceptual structure in language or research on it can fall. The focus and methodology of any specific cognitive-semantic study may then largely represent a particular selection from these entries. In fact, a potential advantage of the taxonomy might be to reveal combinations of the entries that are understudied.

To provide an overview, the taxonomy is first presented in table form. The table represents up to three levels, marked from high to low by upper-case letters, numbers, and lower-case letters. Each level appears with increasing indentation. If the entries at a given level are short, they are placed on the same line to save space, rather than each on a separate line. The discussion in Parts 1 to 11 often presents distinctions still more granular than the lowest level indicated in the table. There, the fourth level is again indicated by numbers.

TABLE 1   Taxonomy of cognitive semantics

A. Major language divisions—The four main compartments of language
   1. Form   2. Grammar   3. Meaning (semantics / pragmatics)   4. Context
B. Participant structure—the sending vs. receiving of a communication
   1. Participant types   2. Participant numbers   3. Participant directionality
C. Arenas of assembly—the venues in which meaning-associated units come together
   1. Inventory   2. Expression   3. Part inventory part expression
D. Content structuring mechanisms—the major systems by which language structures conceptual content
   1. Closed-class semantics—the conceptual "schematic systems" represented by explicit or implicit elements of grammar
      a. Configurational structure   b. Perspective   c. Attention
      d. Force dynamics   e. Cognitive state   f. Reality status
      g. Communicative purpose   h. Role semantics   i. Quantity   j. Ontology
   2. Content patterning—the patterns in which the conceptual continuum is partitioned and arranged
      a. In the morpheme   b. In the lexicon   c. In expression
   3. Content selection—whether/which content is expressed by a speaker
      a. Inclusion vs. omission   b. Alternatives for inclusion
      c. Constraints on selection
   4. Content inference—The hearer infers conceptual content additional to what is explicit
   5. Context—constraints from, e.g., linguistic/thematic/physical/interlocutory/epistemic/social circumstances
   6. Interaction—the structuring of content through cross-participant accommodation
      a. Cross-consideration   b. Turn taking

TABLE 1   Taxonomy of cognitive semantics (*cont.*)

E. Combination—the patterns in which linguistic elements can combine
    1. Additive   2. Operational   3. Idiomatic   4. Constructively discrepant
F. Diachronic comparison—comparing conceptual structures in a single language across different points of its temporal continuum
    1. Long time scale   2. Medium time scale   3. Short time scale
G. Crosslinguistic comparison—comparing conceptual structures across different (varieties of) languages
    1. Scope of comparison   2. Absolutely universal   3. Typological
    4. Repertorial   5. Indefinitely diverse
H. Quantity of manifestation—(changes in) the amount of conceptual content that is represented or occurs
    1. Elaboratedness—the comprehensiveness and granularity of conceptual content
       a. In a communication system   b. In a language user   c. In a lexicon
       d. In expression
    2. Prevalence—the frequency of occurrence of conceptual content
       a. Compared across languages   b. In a single language
I. Communication systems—the use of different channels based on the mode of the sender's production and the receiver's perception
    1. Co-speech gesture   2. Signed language
J. Relations across cognitive faculties—how language relates to other cognitive systems
    1. Language's external relations to other cognitive faculties
       a. Noncommonality of organization   b. Commonality of organization
    2. Language's internal relations to other cognitive faculties
       a. Faculties underlying morphemes   b. Faculties underlying extended communication   c. Faculties underlying certain semantic distinctions
       d. Limitations on faculty coordination
K. Research characteristics—the methodologies and other aspects of approach that shape a language study

The aim of the discussion that follows is to balance the overview character of the table above with enough detail and illustration to make its categories recognizable. To this end, each Part below generally presents a variety of linguistic phenomena to show the range of application of the category it is describing. Throughout, bracketed numbers refer to particular sections in the book. A speaker is referred to as "she" and the hearer as "he".

The fact that the taxonomy is an overview of an entire field prevents citing most work in the area, so that only a small subset of relevant references is provided. However, a personal advantage of the taxonomy is that it has provided a grid over which elements of my own work can be located, and many of these are indicated at pertinent points. the letter T followed by a number from 1 to 16 gives the publication ("T" plus this number are shown as well in the references section), the letter "c" plus a number gives the chapter, and the letter "s" plus a number gives the section.

The eleven main categories of the taxonomy are presented in the next eleven Parts. Space limitations have required the omission of several further categories, but one of these, evolution, is addressed in T13.

1 Major Language Divisions (A)

Language as a whole is traditionally partitioned into three main divisions: form, grammar, and meaning. To this, we here add: context. These divisions are not wholly independent but in part interrelate. Accordingly, though cognitive semantics focuses on meaning, it readily brings in the other divisions where they relate to meaning.

1.1 *Form (A1)*

Form in spoken language rests at base on vocally produced sound. Five types of form might be recognized. One type, "vocal dynamics", is wholly gradient and includes pitch, loudness, speed, timbre, and precision of articulation (T13 s2.2.1). In any given language, three further types consist of discrete elements in specific arrangements and conform to certain universal constraints. These are phonetic distinctive features, phonology, and morphemic shape. And a fifth type of form, intonation, within any given language is a closed class of sentence-spanning sequential patterns consisting mainly of different relative pitches and loudnesses, themselves in part gradient and in part discrete.

1.2 *Grammar (A2)*

To characterize it in a first approximation, grammar consists of all closed-class morphemes. Excluded from grammar then are both open-class morphemes and closed-class linguistic phenomena other than morphemes such as phonological phenomena like distinctive features and phonemes. Because of their significance in this taxonomy, the notions of morpheme, closed class, and open class are expanded on next.

1.2.1 Morpheme (A2a)

The term "morpheme" here refers to any minimal linguistic construct that is associated with a concept—its "meaning". "Minimal" here indicates that even if the construct has components with their own associated concepts, these do not combine to form the construct's overall meaning. Because our analysis bases grammar on morphemes and morphemes on meaning, the division of grammar cannot be fully characterized apart from that of meaning.

The linguistic construct here considered to be a morpheme can be divided into three groups, each with its own types. In group-1, a morpheme has phonological substance. In one type within this group, the morpheme is a particular sequence of segmental phonemes (potentially with suprasegmental tone or stress), like that in *flask* expressing the concept 'narrow-necked bottle'. In another type, it is an intonation pattern, like the singsong contour expressing the concept 'mock threat' that can be used in *I'm gonna tickle you!*. In yet another type, it is a suprasegmental element, like heightened stress on a constituent (indicated throughout this book by an exclamation point before the constituent), representing the concept and the operation of a 'correction', as in *No, I was in !-Paris, not !-London*. In a further type, it is reduplication, like the whole-word iteration in *My many many heavy heavy philosophy books* representing the concept 'very'. And in a still further type, it is an idiom, like *have it in for* which expresses the concept 'nurse a grudge against'. A complex like this last case, though composed of what would otherwise be morphemes themselves, is a morpheme in its own right because its meaning cannot be derived from their meanings.

In group-2, a morpheme does not itself have phonological substance but is (part of) a pattern involving morphemes that do have phonology, a pattern largely based on affordances or constraints on their cooccurrence. As with all morphemes, such a pattern morpheme is associated with a concept. In one type within this group, the morpheme is a particular constituent order (i.e., word order), such as auxiliary before subject, as in *had I known*, expressing the concept 'if'. In another type, the morpheme is a null form lacking overt phonology but posited because, in parallel cases at the same syntactic site, phonological forms do occur—like the zero ending on some nouns instead of the usual *-s*, indicating the concept 'plural', as in *those sheep*.

And the third type includes the remaining grammatical constructs, such as lexical (sub)category and grammatical relation. Thus, the lexical category "adjective", as exhibited by *blue* in *blue hat*, is associated with the concept 'attribute' [4.1.10]. The lexical subcategory "common", as exhibited by the noun *hat*, is associated with the concept 'nonunique'. And the grammatical relation of "direct object", as exhibited by *plum* in *I ate the plum*, is prototypically associated with the concept 'affected Patient'.

Group-3 has one type, that of a complex construction, where a morpheme is a composite that generally includes both phonological morphemes and morphemic patterns but that has an overall meaning not derivable from those of its components. An example is the construction seen in *Could you pass the salt?*, expressing a request by the speaker to the hearer [5.3].[1]

1.2.2 Closed Class (A2b)

A closed class in any given language is a formally distinguishable set with few members that it is difficult to add to. Our concern here is with those closed classes whose members are (largely) concept-associated morphemes.

Within group-1 of morphemes [1.2.1], three of the types are closed-class. First, perhaps every language has a small and relatively fixed set of intonation contours over a sentence, each with an associated concept or polysemous set of concepts. Second, any concept-associated suprasegmental morphemes in a language, like that of heightened stress in English, constitute a closed class, potentially with just one member. And third, any morphemically distinct uses of reduplication in a language are limited within a closed class. As for the two remaining types of morphemes—segmental and idiomatic—they seemingly always include closed classes, whether free like prepositions and conjunctions or bound like inflections and derivations. The rest of the morphemes in these two types, though, fall into one or more open classes [1.2.3].

Within group-2, seemingly every language's set of constituent orders, null forms, and grammatical features (e.g., lexical categories and grammatical relations) constitutes a closed class. As noted, the supposition here is that every member within each of these group-2 closed classes is a morpheme with an associated concept or polysemous set of concepts, however general. For example, within German's closed class of constituent orders, the final positioning of the tensed verb in a syntactically subordinate clause can be interpreted as a morpheme associated with the concept that the clause's event is conceptually subordinated to a main event. This supposition would be faulted, however, if it is determined that a particular language has certain constituent orders, null forms, or grammatical features that simply lack all conceptual associations. In that case, though, the original characterization of grammar as consisting of all closed-class morphemes would be shifted to its consisting of all closed classes with some concept-associated morphemes.

---

1 In the wide application it has here, our term "morpheme" is close to the "construction" of construction grammar (e.g., Fillmore et el., 1988; Goldberg, 1995). In turn, the term "construction" is here mainly reserved for a complex like the one just seen for requesting.

In the third group, finally, every language has complex constructions that can incorporate members from any of the preceding types of closed classes as well as particular open-class morphemes. Each such construction is itself a morpheme associated with a concept. But it may well be that, in every language, such complex constructions themselves constitute a closed class.

1.2.3 Open Class (A2c)

An open class in any given language is a formally distinguishable set with many members that can be readily added to. Though perhaps applicable to other phenomena such as a polysemous range, the term is mainly applied to segmental morphemes and idioms. Within the former of these, an open class can consist of the roots of nouns, verbs, adjectives, or ideophones, where a language includes such distinctions. Open-class morphemes can be associated with certain closed classes such as that of lexical category but, apart from this, they are not in themselves part of grammar.

1.2.4 Morpheme Types within Multimorphemic Words (A2d)

The morphemic types in the first two groups of [1.2.1] were mainly characterized as free forms, but they can also be characterized word-internally under morphology. While syntax mainly addresses the combination of mono- and multimorphemic words into phrases, clauses, and sentences, morphology addresses the combination of morphemes into multimorphemic words in the languages that have them. We here consider multimorphemic words consisting of an open-class morpheme as the root and one or more closed-class morphemes as bound affixes.

Within group-1, morphemes of the segmental type clearly occur for both root and affix, as in *retest*. Idioms also occur, whether involving root and affix as in English *considerable*, 'fairly great in amount', or involving just affixes, as where Atsugewi *-tip* 'out of liquid' and *-u·* 'along an extended path' together in sequence mean 'into a large hole in the ground'. Morphemes of the suprasegmental type occur as well, as where nominalization and its semantics are represented in English by a shift of stress from the second syllable of a verb to the first syllable of the noun (*insúlt → ínsult*). And reduplication occurs, as in representing the aorist and its semantics in classical Greek. But it is unclear whether the morpheme type consisting of an intonation contour has a counterpart within multimorphemic words.

For group-2 morpheme types in a multimorphemic word, we first look at the morphological pattern of Atsugewi, whose polysynthetic verb consists of a "slot" for the verb root surrounded by up to some dozen prefixal and suffixal slots in a fixed order. The lexical category type of morpheme carries over here in that each slot is a distinct type of constituent representing its own semantic category. Thus, the slot immediately before that of the verb root is the "instrumental" constituent representing the event that causes the event expressed by the verb root. Further, inflectional affixes in the polysynthetic word indicate certain grammatical relations—another group-2 type of morpheme.

English arguably exhibits the null type of morpheme. Analogous to the suffix *-en* that converts the adjective *wide* into the verb *widen* is a zero suffix that would convert the adjective narrow into what would be a multimorphemic verb *narrow-Ø* (*The gap widened / narrowed*). And different constituent orders correlate with different semantics in *preunbutton*, which means 'before some event, reverse a buttoning', as against *unprebutton*, which means 'reverse a buttoning done before some event' (though it is unclear that this difference can be given morphemic status).

1.2.5 Contrasting Open- and Closed-Class Status (A2e)

Within group-2 [1.2.1], the grammatical-construct type of morpheme includes an additional grammatical category. It is "state of openness", whose two members are the open-class status and the closed-class status that a morpheme can have. As usual, this further morpheme (the new grammatical category) is associated with a concept: 'the function served in an expression's representation of a meaning'. The function of an open-class morpheme is to contribute to the conceptual content of an expression's meaning, whereas that of a closed-class morpheme is to contribute to its conceptual structure.

For example, in the overall meaning of the sentence *A rustler lassoed the steers*, most of the conceptual content comes from the three open-class morphemes, *rustle*, *lasso*, *steer*. But this content is conceptually structured by the closed-class morphemes in the sentence: *a*; *-er*; *-ed*; *the*; *-s*; the lexical category of "noun" for *rustler / steers* and of "verb" for *lassoed*; the grammatical relation of "subject" for *a rustler* and of "direct object" for the steers; the subject-verb-object constituent order; and the declarative intonation pattern (T1 c1).

It can be noted that my work has systematically used the term "conceptual content" in both a more specific and a more general sense. Its specific sense, used in the present example, contrasts with "conceptual structure". But its general sense refers to the entirety of a meaning, covering both structure and specific-sense content. This book uses both senses, distinguished by context.

1.3 *Meaning (A3)*

Meaning in language consists of conceptual content associated with linguistic form or grammar. Such meaning can then be divided into semantics and pragmatics.

As for semantics, by one analysis, it initially refers to those conceptual associations that are preestablished in a language and hence in the language's lexicon. Semantics here then consists of the conceptual complexes associated with morphemes of any of the types presented in [1.2]. In addition, semantics refers to combinations of such associations in a multimorphemic word or an expression.

Pragmatics, on the other hand, refers to conceptual content that a hearer—through world knowledge, association, or inference—adds to what is directly (i.e., semantically) present in a speaker's expression.

We can illustrate with the sentence *The goblet of wine slowly went around the banquet table* (T12 s1.6.1). A hearer might first process this sentence so as to form a "direct semantic" conception of a goblet moving along a closed-circuit path near a table's perimeter. He might further form an "immediate pragmatic" conception of the goblet successively passed from hand to hand by diners adjacently seated at the table's perimeter. And he might then form a "further pragmatic" conception of the event as the custom of a social order that the diners are members of, where each in turn sips the wine as part of a ritual.

Cognitive-semantic research largely focuses on the meaning division of language. It brings in form and grammar mainly for their relation to such meaning. This is a balance reflected in this taxonomy.

1.4   Context (A4)

For any component of an utterance, the "speech-external" context consists of everything interlocutory, physical, social, and cultural in the environment that surrounds the utterance. And the "speech-internal" context consists of other components in the current or surrounding utterances. In both cases, the relevance of any portion of the context decreases with its spatial and/or temporal distance.

Every language has a certain special set of morphemes belonging to group-1. Each morpheme in this set is lexicalized to form a link from itself in an utterance to an element in the context. Traditionally, a morpheme in this set that links to a speech-external vs. a speech-internal contextual element is respectively called a "deictic" and an "anaphor". But to foreground their common properties, (T12) calls a morpheme of either kind a "trigger". The contextual element it links to in turn is called its "target".

Thus, the trigger that acts as a deictic when a speaker points to an object in a display case and says *That's the new iPhone* but acts as an anaphor when the speaker says *The new iPhone is out—that's what I'd like for Christmas*. The target in both cases is an iPhone, but it is a physical object in the speech-external case and the referent of a word in the speech-internal case.

2 Participant Structure (B)

A communication has certain participants in its execution—a sender that produces it and a receiver that interprets it. Such production [4.3] and interpretation [4.4] engage different cognitive processes in the structuring of conceptual content. A cognitive-semantic study can involve the one, the other, or both participants—or neither if the subject of analysis is judged to be neutral to the distinction.

A study can also focus on any of the alternatives distinguished next.

2.1 *Participant Type (B1)*
A communication can occur in different modalities [9], and the terms for its participants can vary accordingly. Thus in English, the sender can be a speaker, signer, gesturer, or writer, while the corresponding receiver is a hearer, sign viewer, gesture viewer, or reader. For ease, though, the discussion here largely refers only to speakers and hearers.

Receivers can be divided along a further parameter. An addressee is one to whom the speaker has overtly directed her communication, while a bystander has perceived the communication otherwise. And a bystander can be further subdivided into an incidental type and an "indirect addressee", where the speaker tailors her communication to function as a message to him.

2.2 *Participant Numbers (B2)*
A communication may prototypically have one sender and one receiver but can readily diverge from this pattern. Thus, a producer can lack an addressee, as with internal speech. Two individuals can function as a single speaker as when completing each other's sentences while addressing a third person. And a sender can have multiple receivers, as in public speaking or published writing.

2.3 *Participant Directionality (B3)*
A communication can proceed in just one direction, as in the last two cases. Or it can proceed in both directions with the participants alternating their roles, as in written correspondence or in verbal turn taking [4.6.2].

3 Arenas of Assembly (C)

A cognitive-semantic study can address a language's basic meaning-associated units individually or as they are assembled in either of two arenas: the inventory or the expression. An inventory consists of preestablished elements in the language in a structured atemporal collection, while an expression consists of elements selected from the inventory by a speaker and placed in a structured temporal sequence.

3.1 Inventory (C1)

At any given time in its history, a language has a fixed inventory of elements—its lexicon or construction—that a speaker must learn. This inventory includes all morphemes—that is, its minimal concept-associated constructs [1.2]—numbering in the thousands. And it includes any morphological and syntactic structures or processes that might not be considered morphemes. It also includes all nonproductive combinations of such elements. To illustrate this last case with combinations of English adjectives and affixes that derive adjectives into nouns, it includes *legality, warmth, freedom*, and *bravery* but not **legalth, *warmity, *freery*, or **bravedom*.

A research study might address the whole inventory. Or it might address any of innumerable subinventories that are characterized formally and/or semantically. A formally based subinventory might vary quantitatively with greater or lesser size, like that of open-class morphemes and that of mass nouns, respectively. Or it could vary qualitatively like the sets of affixes that make up different inflectional paradigms. A semantically based subinventory in turn might consist of those morphemes whose meanings include a semantic component of path or negation, or of those whose meanings are judged to be universal. And a subinventory defined both formally and semantically might consist of Manner verbs or topicalizing constructions.

3.2 Expression (C2)

In the arena of expression, a speaker selects elements from her language's lexicon and joins them temporally in a nonce formation. This process can occur over the scope of a single multimorphemic word, as with the six morphologically assembled morphemes in the word *unredirtiably*, or over the scope of a syntactically assembled sentence, as in *This high-tech polish has made my counter unredirtiably clean*.

3.3 Part Inventory, Part Expression (C3)

A language generally has numerous temporal assemblies of morphemes that are not idioms—their overall meanings arise compositionally from their components—but that occur so frequently that they, as it were, have honorary status as members of the lexicon. Such "collocations" straddle both the arenas of expression and inventory. They can occur over the scope of a single multimorphemic word like *unforgettable*; over that of a phrase like *every last vestige of*; over that of a clause like *I never cease to be amazed (that S / at NP)*; or over that of a complex sentence, like the formulation *just because S1, (it) doesn't mean S2*, as in *Just because their lights are on, (it) doesn't mean they're home*.

The effect at work in such partial lexicalizing is called "entrenchment" by Langacker (1987) and "unitization", "routinization", or "automatization" in the psychological literature.

4 Content Structuring Mechanisms (D)

Language has certain major mechanisms, that is, extensive organized systems, that function to structure conceptual content. Six such mechanisms are proposed next.

4.1 Closed-Class Semantics (D1)

A principal mechanism by which language structures conceptual content is closed-class semantics. The closed-class morphemes that occur across languages, as characterized in [1.2.2], largely represent conceptual complexes that function to structure conceptual content.

An analysis of these conceptual complexes can be characterized in four stages. First, these complexes can be broken down into basic "semantic components". Second, these semantic components can be gathered together from languages around the world into a single inventory. Third, semantic components can be grouped together into a smaller number of "conceptual categories". And fourth, these categories can be grouped together into a still smaller number of large-scale "schematic systems".

Each of these three levels—those of semantic components, conceptual categories, and schematic systems—has semantic constraints on its elements. Accordingly, the set of elements at each level is mostly closed and each set is a universally available "repertory" [7.3].

This entire three-level hierarchy is one of language's most fundamental conceptual structuring systems.

In accord with some principle of representativeness, every language draws its own subset from this hierarchy, consisting of certain semantic components together with their particular conceptual categories and schematic systems. It assembles these into the conceptual complexes represented by its closed-class morphemes. These together provide the language with a local conceptual structuring system of its own.

The following discussion is organized in terms of the ten large-scale schematic systems that have been reliably determined. The first four were proposed in (T1), while the remaining six are newly proposed here.

4.1.1 Configurational Structure (D1a)
In the schematic system of configurational structure, closed-class morphemes represent delineations—often geometric-like structures or schemas—in space, time, quality, or other ontological domains.

4.1.1.1 *In Space (D1a1)*
For space, the closed-class representation of configurational structure is provided by satellites and/or adpositions and/or noun affixes, together with a range of adverbial expressions.

These can conceptually partition a scene into three components—a Figure, a Ground, and potentially a secondary reference entity. The Figure is a moving or conceptually movable entity whose site, path, or orientation is conceived as a variable whose particular value is the relevant issue. The Ground is a reference entity with respect to which the Figure's variables are characterized. The secondary reference entity is a grid or viewpoint with respect to which the Figure or Ground can be further spatially characterized.

To illustrate, such scene partitioning is exhibited by a closed-class preposition like *above*, as in *The light bulb is above the radio*. Here, the Figure is the lightbulb, the Ground is the radio, and the secondary reference entity is the vertical axis of the earth-based grid. The preposition characterizes the Figure as located on the same vertical axis as the Ground in a positive direction from it.

Constraints on the universally available semantic inventory limit the closed-class representation of space to only certain conceptual categories and, within them, to only a few semantic components (T4). Thus, the conceptual category of "number" includes only the four semantic components of one, two, several, and many—never: even, odd, dozen—and there are English prepositions requiring a particular one of those components for the Ground, as seen respectively in *The basketball lay near the boulder / between the boulders / among the boulders / amidst the cornstalks*. The conceptual category of "motility" has two semantic components, stationary and moving—never: fixedly vs. temporarily stationary—as represented by the prepositions in *I stayed at / went into the library*. The conceptual category of bounding has two semantic components, unbounded and bounded—never: gradient transitional zone—as in *I walked along the shore (for 5 minutes) / I walked the-length-of the pier (in 10 minutes)*.

And the conceptual category of "contour" has only four semantic components, straight, arced, circular, and meandering—never: spiral, zigzag, square—as in *I walked across the plain / over the hill / around the flagpole/ about the town*.

In their type of geometry, spatial closed-class specifications are preponderantly topological, abstracted away from such Euclidean specifics as size, contour, and angle. Thus, in its requirements for the Ground, the preposition *in* is magnitude neutral—*in a thimble / volcano*; shape-neutral—*in a well / trench*; continuity-neutral—*in a bell jar / bird cage*; and closure-neutral—*in a beach ball / punch bowl* (the last two properties exceed those of mathematical topology). And in its requirements for the Figure's path, the preposition *through* is magnitude-neutral—*I walked through the garden /forest*; and shape-neutral—*I walked straight / in a zigzag through the forest*.

Further, closed-class specifications are generally neutral to whether a spatial element is "factive" or "fictive"—that is, whether it exists physically or only imaginarily (T1 c2). This is seen for the path respectively in *The barrel rolled / The fence runs from the plateau down into the valley*.

English has an extensive system of "spatial augments" (T12 s6.4.3) that characterize a factive or fictive path to a location represented by a following NP. The syntax of the system is shown in (1) and its semantics in (2). Each augment is optional, but if two or more are selected, they occur in the order shown. A maximum of perhaps five out of the ten augments can be selected at once, with different combinations having different degrees of felicity.

(1) (right) (way/just) (back) (on) (off) (up/down) (over) (Sat) (P) (Augs) NP.

(2)
 a. right: 'directly (without detour), immediately (without delay)', 'exactly (without wider compass), specifically (none other than)'
 b. way/just: 'distally' / 'proximally'
 c. back: 'along a path progressing to a location that was previously departed from'; 'along a path to the rear of a reference object'
 d. on: 'in resumption or continuation of a previous path'; 'without reserve'
 e. off: 'along a path (obliquely) away from a reference point'
 f. up/down: 'along a path progressing vertically against/with the direction of gravity'
 g. over: 'along a path progressing horizontally'
 h. Sat: a conformational satellite (e.g., *in, out* 'along a path entering/leaving an enclosure')
 i. P: a preposition (e.g., *to, from, of*)
 j. Augs: one or more of a certain subset of the preceding spatial augments (e.g., *up in*)

A TAXONOMY OF COGNITIVE SEMANTICS   15

The formula accounts for elaborate spatial expressions like those in (3). Thus, in (3a), the *right*, the *back*, and the *down* respectively represent the (2a, c, and f) terms, while the *out*, the *from*, and the sequence *up in* respectively represent the (2 h, i, and j) terms.

(3) a. Come right back down out from up in there! (e.g., said by a parent to a child in a tree house)
     b. I'm way off over here. (e.g., shouted by a child in a field to a parent in a farmhouse)
     c. The vacuum cleaner is just down around behind the clothes hamper.
     d. She crawled on out along the branch.

4.1.1.2   *In Time (D1a2)*

For time, configurational structure has closed-class representation by the same types of grammatical elements as for space, with the addition of tense markers, subordinating conjunctions, and adverbial pro-clauses [4.1.8 (D1h4)]. It conceptually partitions an episode into the same three components, but now the Figure is an event whose temporal location is the relevant issue, the Ground is a reference event with a known temporal location with respect to which the Figure's temporal location is characterized, and the secondary reference entity is the timeline or a viewpoint along it.

To illustrate, such episode partitioning is exhibited by a closed-class subordinating conjunction like *after*, as in *I went home after I shopped*. Here, the Figure is the event of going home, the Ground is the event of shopping, and the secondary reference entity is the timeline. The Figure here must lie on the time line in a positive direction from the Ground without overlap (T1 c6).

As noted, episode partitioning is also effected by a closed-class morpheme that marks tense, like the *-ed* in *I walked away*. Here, though, the Ground is not a specified event but the moment at which the morpheme is uttered (T12 c11).

4.1.1.3   *In Quality (D1a3)*

In referring to a quality, configurational structure is seen in the "axial properties" of certain closed-class morphemes (T1 c1)—for example, of *somewhat* and *almost* in construction with adjectives like *sick* and *well*. Acceptable combinations here are *He is somewhat sick / He is almost well*, but unacceptable are **He is somewhat well / *He is almost sick* (in the intended sense). This acceptability pattern rests on the schema for 'health'. This schema is a geometric ray consisting of a point and an unbounded line extending from it, where *well* refers to the point and *sick* to the line. Then *somewhat* indicates a fictive path from the point to a location along the line a short distance away, while *almost* indicates a fictive path from a location further out along the line back to a location closer to the point.

4.1.1.4   Across Domains (D1a4)

A number of conceptual categories within configurational structure apply to more than one domain, thus showing a commonality of conceptual structuring (T1 c1). For example, the conceptual category of "plexity" with its two main members, the semantic components "uniplex" and "multiplex", is in play where certain closed-class morphemes represent respectively the singular or plural occurrence of a noun's referent in space while others represent the semelfactive or iterated occurrence of a verb's referent in time. And the conceptual category of "bounding" with its two main members "bounded" and "unbounded" is at work where certain closed-class morphemes respectively represent the count or mass status of a noun's referent in space while others represent the telicity or atelicity in the aspect of a verb's referent in time.

4.1.2   Perspective (D1b)

In the schematic system of perspective, closed-class morphemes determine the location, distance, or motility of a perspective point from which a referent scene is to be conceptualized (T1 c1).

For example, the location of the perspective point within the scene represented by *The lunchroom door opened and two men walked in* must be inside the lunchroom, but is outside it or neutral in *Two men opened the lunchroom door and walked in*. In accord with certain English rules, the difference arises from the closed-class factor of whether the initial verb's subject is its Patient (the door) or its Agent (the men).

With regard to distance and motility, the perspective point is distal and stationary in the scene represented by *There were some houses in the valley*, whereas it is proximal and moving for the same scene when represented by *There was a house every now and then through the valley*. This distinction is effected by the following closed-class differences: plural vs. singular subject number, a construction representing spatial vs. temporal distribution, and a static vs. dynamic preposition.

4.1.3   Attention (D1c)

In the schematic system of attention, closed-class morphemes direct greater and lesser degrees of attention to different aspects of a referent situation (T1 c1, T6, T15 s1.2.1).

One such aspect involves reference to a multiplexity of entities. Here, English has numerous pairs of closed-class constructions that direct greater attention either to the full complement of the entities en masse or to a single exemplar representative of the set (T1 c1). Instances of such full-complement/exemplar pairs are shown in (4) where the entities are doctors serving as the subject of a sentence whose predicate might be *can/could be reasoned with*.

(4) doctors / a doctor (generic)   many doctors / many a doctor   hardly any doctors / hardly a (single) doctor
all doctors / every doctor   some doctors here and there / a doctor here and there   no doctors / no (nary a) doctor.
all the doctors / each doctor   doctors one after another / one doctor after another

For another aspect of attention (T15 s7.1.3), the closed-class grammatical relation of subjecthood generally directs greater attention to the referent with that status than to other nominal referents. Thus, in *The landlord rented the apartment to the tenant*, the owner as subject is more salient than the user as oblique object, and as such may evoke thoughts of collateral actions by him such as preparing the apartment for new occupancy, advertising it, and interviewing interested parties. But in *The tenant rented the apartment from the landlord*, the user as subject is now more salient, and as such may evoke thoughts of collateral actions like checking publicized listings and visiting other vacancies.

4.1.4   Force Dynamics (D1d)

In the schematic system of force dynamics, closed-class morphemes represent a framework of patterns in which one entity exerts force on another. These patterns include the exertion of force, resistance to such exertion, the overcoming of such resistance, the prevention of a force, and the removal of such prevention. Hence, they can represent causing, letting, helping, hindering, blocking, and unblocking (T1 c7).

Two of the basic steady-state patterns, the extended causing and the hindering of motion, are seen respectively in *The ball rolled on because of the wind / despite the stiff grass*. Here, the closed-class forms representing force dynamics are *on*, *because of*, and *despite*.[2] The ball in the first case has a tendency toward

---

2   Force dynamics in the predicate can be represented not only by the closed-class satellite *on* but also by the verb *keep* (keep rolling), which is presently open-class but seems amenable to grammaticalization.

rest which the stronger wind overcomes, but in the second case it has a tendency toward motion that overcomes weaker opposition from the grass.

The closed class of modals largely represents force-dynamic patterns as well. Thus, *should*, as in *She should lock her door*, pits the speaker's values as to what is good and beliefs as to what is beneficial against the subject's contrary behavior. And *dare*, as in *He dare not leave the house*, opposes the subject's courage against external threat.

4.1.5 Cognitive State (D1e)

In the schematic system of cognitive state, closed-class forms represent certain psychological conditions in a sentient individual. Such states largely fall into four categories: knowledge, expectation, intention, and affect.

4.1.5.1 *Knowledge (D1e1)*

A major category of cognitive state with grammatical representation is an individual's state of knowledge—possessing or lacking it.

Speaker's Lack of Knowledge. In using a question construction, as in *Who was at the party?*, a speaker indicates a lack of knowledge on her part that she wants the hearer to fill in. Or again, some epistemic modals indicate the speaker's lack of definite knowledge about the proposition, as *may* does in *The tower may have collapsed in the earthquake*.

Speaker's Both Having and Lacking Knowledge. Additionally, some constructions represent a pattern of a speaker's both knowing and not knowing. An example involving disjunction is *Either Wayne or Rose spoke next*, where the speaker knows that one of those two spoke but does not know which one. An example involving a conditional construction is *If Lynne presided, then the meeting ended on time*. Here, the speaker does not know who in fact presided, but does know that, of the alternative possibilities, the one in which Lynne presides finishes punctually. And a quantitative example is seen in *at least*, as in *At least a hundred people came*, where the speaker knows that a hundred people did come but does not know whether any above that number came.

Hearer's State of Knowledge. A speaker's choice between a definite and an indefinite determiner can represent her assessment of the hearer's state of knowledge. Thus, in saying *I fed the cat*, the speaker judges that the hearer knows (can readily identify) the particular cat. But in saying *I fed a cat*, she judges that the hearer does not know the particular cat.

4.1.5.2 *Expectation (D1e2)*

Another grammatically represented conceptual category of cognitive state is expectation. This is an individual's relatively strong belief that a certain outcome was or is to occur. Constructions expressing expectation can present the outcome as either known or unknown.

Known Outcome. A construction can represent a known outcome but can further evoke a sense of confirmation if the outcome conforms with an expectation and of surprise if it does not. For example, the closed-class conjunctions *and* and *but* respectively mark their clause as being confirmingly in or surprisingly out of accord with prior expectation. A possible example is *He knocked on her door and/but her husband answered*. This distinction is an English realization of the general expectational category of "mirativity".

Or again, certain interrogative or negative constructions indicate strong surprise at a known outcome contrary to expectation. Thus, a speaker at a party, on spotting an old friend she has not seen for years, might exclaim *Is that really you?!* or *It can't be you!*.

Closed-class morphemes can also represent expectation about the time at which one condition shifts to its opposite. Thus, *still*, as in *The snake is still lying there*, indicates that stationariness is lasting longer than the speaker had expected before a shift to motion. And *at last*, as in *The snake is moving at last*, indicates the same expectation except that the shift is now actual. But *already*, as in *The snake is already moving*, indicates that the shift is sooner than the speaker had expected.

An expectation can also pertain to quantity, where closed-class morphemes represent a known outcome with (surprisingly) more or less than expected of some factor. The "less" case is seen in *Only Sue sang*, where it was expected that others would sing as well. The "more" case is seen in *Even Trent sang*, where *even* ranks a set of entities along an expectational hierarchy and indicates the participation of the least expected one in addition to that of the others.

Where the quantity involves a specific number, English has closed-class representation indicating that a figure below, above, or exactly that number is more or less than what was expected. This is shown in (5), where the forms might appear initially in a sentence that continues: *people came to the play*.

(5)
	below 100	**exactly 100**	**above 100**
more than expected	almost 100	as many as 100	more than 100
less than expected	fewer than 100	only 100	barely 100

Unknown Outcome. Though the future is in principle always unknown, an event in it can be expected. Such expectation is indicated by the closed-class particle *yet*, as in *The governor is not implicated in the scandal yet*. It is also indicated by the closed-class conjunction *when*—in contrast with the expectationally neutral *if*—as in *We'll watch the movie when/if they come*.³

For some constructions, the expected unknown is not an outcome but a state of affairs occurring at any time. Thus, in contrast with a simple yes/no question like *Is she in college now?*, a tag question indicates the speaker's expectation that the polarity of the main clause is correct, as seen both in *She's in college now, isn't she?* and in *She isn't in college now, is she?*. Comparably, in a question based on antonymous adjectives referring to a scale, the adjective for the scale's higher portion is expectationally neutral, as in *How long is the crosspiece?*. But the adjective for the scale's lower portion indicates an expectation of a lower value, as in *How short is the crosspiece?*.

4.1.5.3   *Intention (D1e3)*

Closed-class morphemes can further represent the cognitive state of intention—an Agent's aim that certain actions she performs will lead to a desired outcome. Again, it can be either known or unknown whether this outcome has occurred.

Unknown Outcome. Where the Agent is the subject, the particle *to* with the infinitive can introduce her intended outcome, one whose realization is unknown. An example is *She broke open the bone to get at the marrow*.

Or again, the grammatical relation of indirect object status as well as the preposition *for*—as in *I'm buying Jane a cake / a cake for Jane*—indicate the subject's intention to give, while the preposition *for*, as in *I'm buying a cake for the party*, indicates the intention to provide. It is moot here whether the Patient was actually delivered.

Further, a deictic demonstrative, like the *there* in *You can hang your coat over there*—accompanied by a targeting gesture [9.1.1]—expresses the speaker's intention that the hearer join his attention with her own on a particular target (here, a certain location), though it is moot whether he actually does so.

Known Outcome. Many languages have different constructions or inflections indicating whether a known event was intended by the subject or is accidental. English lacks such means. Thus, from *I broke my arm* it is known that my arm is broken, but it is unknown whether I did or did not intend this outcome.

---

3   An expected outcome that is relatively future to a past event but is still before the present can be taken either as known or unknown. An example of the known case is *The governor was not implicated in the scandal yet*. An example of the unknown case is *We were going to watch the movie when/if they came*.

4.1.5.4 Affect (Die4)

Closed-class morphemes can also represent certain types of affect, another category within cognitive state. For example, a speaker's desire or wish is expressed by the desiderative or optative inflections of some languages as well as by the English constructions in *May she succeed!* and *Would that she succeeds!*. Speaker regret is expressed by another construction, that in *If only I had entered the contest!*. The particle *so*, as in *That sequoia is so wide!*, expresses the speaker's amazement at the extremeness of the indicated quality. And the subordinating conjunction, *lest*, as in *They cleared the path lest she trip*, represents the main-clause subject's concern or worry over the potential occurrence of an undesired event.

Closed-class representation of affect is relatively limited in English—the preceding instances of it are mostly uncommon—but it is more extensive in other languages. Thus, in addition to the four types of affect just cited, Yiddish frequently expresses endearedness with its noun suffix *-ele* (e.g., *ketsele* 'kitty'); impatience with its verbal clitic *-zhe* (e.g., *Zog-zhe vos du vilst* 'Do say what you want'); and pity and willfulness with its verb phrase particles *nebekh* (e.g., *Er iz nebekh geshtorbn* 'He alas died') and *dafke* (e.g., *Ikh vil geyn af a lektsie, must du dafke geyn in kino* '(Just when) I want to go to a lecture, you !!- would have to go to a movie').

4.1.6 Reality Status (D1f)

In the schematic system of reality status, closed-class morphemes represent or determine the state or degree of a referent's realization. This schematic system interacts closely with the preceding one, specifically with state of knowledge. Thus, certain types of reality status are known to be realized or to be unrealized, while others have an unknown state of realization.

4.1.6.1 Known as Realized (D1f1)

The main type of known realization—the factual or actual—is largely represented across languages by their indicative declarative constructions with positive polarity in either the past or present, as in English *He danced / is dancing*.

Further, realization can largely be conceptualized as a gradient achieved only to some degree along a one-dimensional scale, and some closed-class forms can specify that degree and indicate that it is known. Thus, *almost*, as in *This peach is almost ripe*, represents a known, mostly complete degree of realization.

And in a performative construction, the speaker causes the specified proposition to become realized by the act of uttering the construction, and thus knows that it is in fact realized. This construction is grammatically indicated in

English by the simple present and optionally by the closed-class form *hereby*, as in *I hereby declare this meeting adjourned*.

4.1.6.2   Known as Unrealized (D1f2)

As for known nonrealization, one main type is simply indicated by a negative, as in *I didn't dance*. Another type appears in counterfactual constructions—as in *I should have danced*, or *I would have danced if I'd had the time*—which express the known fact that I did not dance.

A third type is represented by a future tense construction, as in *I'll bake the apple*, where it is known that the referent event is currently not realized. Languages can have different future constructions based on where the potential event is located on a scale from a simple prediction to a commitment to bring it about.

And the referents of all tropes are known not to be realized as represented literally. However, this fact fits the present schematic system only where closed-class elements signal the presence of the trope. This can be the case with sarcasm, as in *Here comes Mr. Sure-footed*, where the singsong intonation, and the "Mr." before an adjective are the indicators that the stated attribute must be conceptually reversed [5.4.2].

4.1.6.3   Unknown State of Realization (D1f3)

As for unknown reality status, one main type is a yes/no question construction, as in *Did she swallow the pill*, where the speaker does not know a referent event's state of realization and wants the addressee to provide information specifically on that issue (cross-indexed in [4.1.5 (D1e1)]).

Further, without knowing the state of a referent's realization, a speaker can still estimate its probability, indicating this value from lesser to greater with closed-class elements like *just maybe, perhaps* or the epistemic modal *may*, and *likely*, as in *It may have / It likely rained there last night*. In fact, seemingly all epistemic modals represent the speaker's lack of knowledge about the referent's actual realization while providing an estimate of its probability. Thus, the *should* in *Bess should be home by now* indicates that the speaker does not know specifically whether or not Bess is home but estimates it as probable on the basis of other knowledge.

Comparably, "evidentials" other than the factive kind seem to indicate that the speaker does not know the referent's state of realization but infers that it is probable on the basis of certain types of evidence [10.1.1 (J1a1)]. Thus, a speaker of a language with many evidential distinctions might say the equivalent of *Tom must have been in the forest chopping wood*, but, instead of a morpheme for the general evidential 'must', will add a more specific morpheme for the "non-visual perceptual" evidential (e.g., I heard the sound of whacks coming from the forest); for the "periodicity" evidential (e.g., It was 3:00 PM and he usually chops wood at that time); for the "consequence" evidential (e.g., The axe was missing from its usual place on the wall / I see wood chips on the ground); or for the "hearsay" evidential (e.g., I heard that he was out chopping wood).

Reality status is also indicated by certain verb classes and by the class of satellites they can take (T2 c3). Thus, a "moot fulfillment" verb like hunt, as in *The police hunted the fugitive*, indicates that, while such police actions as interrogating witnesses were realized, the intended outcome of finding and capturing the fugitive has unknown realization. However, if the "fulfillment satellite" *down* is added, the outcome is known to have been realized.

4.1.7 Communicative Purpose (D1g)

In the schematic system of communicative purpose, closed-class morphemes indicate the effect that a speaker intends to have on the hearer by communicating with him. Among these effects, the speaker can inform, order, request, question, suggest, warn, correct, and rouse the hearer—all expanded on next.

4.1.7.1 *Informing (D1g1)*

The speaker's seemingly most frequent communicative purpose is to inform the hearer of the proposition being represented—that is, to present certain information to the hearer with the aim that he store it at least in working memory, available for reference in the immediate discourse. This purpose is represented crosslinguistically by declarative constructions, as in English *They signed the petition*.

4.1.7.2 *Ordering (D1g2)*

In ordering, the communicative purpose of the speaker is, through her socially based influence, to induce the hearer, through his own volitional activities, to perform the specified action. Ordering is largely represented by imperative constructions, like the subjectless English construction in *Sign the petition!*.

4.1.7.3 *Requesting (D1g3)*

In requesting, the speaker's communicative purpose is to let the hearer know of some action that she would like the hearer to perform voluntarily. English can represent requesting with what might be called the "modal-request construction", which consists of the interrogative construction with certain modal forms and optionally the particle *please* [5.3]. An example is *Could you (please) sign the petition?*.

4.1.7.4   Questioning (D1g4)

In questioning—represented by closed-class interrogative words and constructions, as in English *Did you sign the petition?* and *Who signed the petition?*, the speaker lacks certain information and her purpose in communicating is to fill that lack by requesting the hearer to provide it verbally. Questioning is thus a subtype of requesting, where the hearer's response is to be verbal. Its effect can accordingly be equaled by a request construction that specifies such a verbal response, as in *Could you please tell me if you signed the petition? / who signed the petition?*.

4.1.7.5   Suggesting (D1g5)

In suggesting, as when represented by specialized constructions like those in *Why not go to Hawaii?* and *How about going to Hawaii?*, the speaker's purpose is to present or advocate for an action that the hearer can consider undertaking as his choice among alternatives.

4.1.7.6   Warning (D1g6)

In warning, a speaker's communicative purpose is to inform the hearer of a potential risk to him that he might therefore want to avoid. Atsugewi has an entire "admonitive" verb conjugation expressing warning, a conceptual area that can extend to mock threat and teasing. An example is /tamlawilcahki/, a verb inflected for 'I' as subject and 'you' as object, that, serving as a mock threat, can be glossed as *I'm going to tickle you*.[4] As seen in [1.2], English has closed-class representation of just such mock threat—a certain singsong intonation contour—which could, for example, be used with the gloss just cited.

4.1.7.7   Correcting (D1g7)

In correcting, the speaker, who believes she has noticed a mistaken reference in the hearer's preceding utterance, provides the correct reference, and her purpose is that the hearer substitute the latter for the former in his cognitive representation (T12 s13.1.2). One closed-class element that English uses for this

---

4   The Atsugewi form might more specifically be rendered as "Better watch out lest I tickle you with this pencil". It consists of the verb root *-wil* 'for flesh to jiggle', the Cause prefix *ra-* 'by acting on the Figure with a linear object moved laterally', the affix complex *m- -cahki* 'I-subject you-object', and the mode prefix *ta-* 'admonitive'.

purpose is heightened stress on a constituent. It here appears on the replacement constituent, as where the hearer first says *I heard you were in London last year* and the speaker responds *No, I was in !-Paris*.

As another example, beside the ordinary closed-class morpheme in French for 'yes', *oui*, is the alternative morpheme *si*, which is lexicalized to correct a mistaken negative polarity in the hearer's prior utterance and replace it with a positive one.

4.1.7.8   *Excitation (D1g8)*
In excitation, the speaker intends to affect the hearer by the intensity of her surprise or wonder at some phenomenon (Michaelis, 2001). This purpose can be represented by closed-class forms like those in *That hawk is so fast! / How fast that hawk is! / What speed that hawk has!*.

A note can be inserted here that this book analyzes cognitive state, reality status, and communicative purpose as distinct schematic systems on semantic grounds. But the traditional linguistic term "mood" has generally covered all three, and indeed languages often use the same closed-class elements to represent more than one of, or combinations of, these systems.

4.1.8   Role Semantics (D1h)
In the schematic system of role semantics, a closed-class morpheme represents the conceptual relation that the referent of one syntactic constituent has to that of another. The two constituents can occur within a phrase, a clause, a complex sentence, or a compound sentence, discussed next in order.

4.1.8.1   *In a Phrase (D1h1)*
The English closed-class possessive *-s*, as in *chef's hat* or *book's cover*, can be cliticized to a noun phrase representing referent A. This combination is then in syntactic construction with a noun phrase representing referent B. The clitic indicates that referent A has the semantic role of a possessor and referent B the semantic role of a possessum in a relationship of possession, that is, where referent B belongs to referent A.

4.1.8.2   *In a Clause (D1h2)*
Within a clause containing a verb and one or more major nominals, closed-class morphemes like constituent order, adpositions, and affixes can indicate that the nominals have such grammatical relations as subject, direct object, indirect object, and oblique object to the clause. The full set of such grammatical relations in a language is itself a closed class. For each of its polysemous senses,

a verb has a certain "syntactic argument structure" that determines which nominals must or may appear with particular grammatical relations. In turn, the referent of each such nominal has a certain semantic role in relation to the event represented by the clause. Together, these referents in their particular semantic roles constitute the verb's "semantic argument structure".

Such roles can be conceived as coarser-grained and potentially universal, like the roles of Agent or Patient, Figure or Ground. Thus, the nominals in *The cyclist threw her helmet onto the bed* refer to entities with the respective semantic roles of Agent, Patient/Figure, and Ground in the event represented by the clause. The referent of the subject nominal (*the cyclist*) has the role of Agent, which here involves acting on the Patient, while the referent of the direct-object nominal (*her helmet*) has the role of Patient, which here involves being acted on by the Agent. The referent of the direct-object nominal also has the role of Figure, which here involves moving along a path relative to the Ground, while the referent of the oblique-object nominal (*the bed*) has the role of Ground, which here involves serving as a reference point with respect to which that path is characterized [4.1.1 (D1a1)].

Alternatively, the semantic roles can be finer-grained and specific to a small set of verbs. Thus, the nominals in *I bought a car from the dealer for $30,000* refer respectively to a person, an object, another person, and money with the roles of a buyer, merchandise, seller, and payment relative to the commercial frame represented by the verb (Fillmore, 1976).

4.1.8.3   *In a Complex Sentence (D1h3)*
Within a complex sentence, subordinating conjunctions are closed-class forms that represent the semantic role of the main clause's event in relation to the subordinate clause's event (T1 c6). Some of these relations can be analyzed under other schematic systems above. Thus, the main-clause event's anteriority, posteriority, and concurrence seen in *I shopped before the sun set / after I jogged / while it snowed* can be treated as temporal schemas under configurational structure [4.1.1 (D1a2)]. And the causality and concession in *The bench is wet because it rained / although I wiped it* can be treated under force dynamics [4.1.4].

But other relations would be treated here alone. These include conditionality, as in *She'll move back here if she loses her job*; counterfactual exceptivity, as in *I'd join you, only I'm feeling tired*; and negative additionality, as in *I can dance no more than I can sing*.

Still further relations are represented by constructions that are not technically complex sentences but are like them in representing two events separately and hierarchically. These include additionality, as in *I was promoted besides (in addition to*) *getting a raise*; substitution (of a less for a more expected event), as in *The wind blew instead of the rain falling*; and covariation, as in *The hotter it is, the worse I feel*.

4.1.8.4   In a Compound Sentence (D1h4)

Within a compound sentence, almost all of the same role relations just seen for complex sentences—though now it is the role of the second clause relative to the first—are represented by closed-class "adverbial pro-clauses" (T1 c6). These are shown in (6) in capitals and with their semantic components. They are the counterparts of all the subordinators of the preceding section except the last one.

(6)   a. The sun set, but FIRST (= before that) I shopped.
     b. I jogged and THEN (= after that) I shopped.
     c. It was snowing, and I shopped THE WHILE (= during that).
     d. It rained, and SO (= because of that) the bench is wet.
     e. I wiped the bench but it was STILL (= despite that) wet.
     f. She might lose her job but THEN (= in that case) she'll move back here.
     g. I'm feeling tired or ELSE (= other than that) I'd join you.
     h. I can't sing, and I can't dance EITHER (= any more than that).
     i. I got a raise and I ALSO (= in addition to that) got promoted.
     j. The rain didn't fall but the wind blew INSTEAD (= instead of that).

4.1.9   Quantity (D1i)

Within the schematic system of quantity, closed-class morphemes represent the number, amount, or degree of a referent. This system, potentially quite extensive in a language, again structures conceptual content. Closed-class elements can represent either a single quantity or a comparison between quantities, as discussed next in order.

4.1.9.1   Single Quantity (D1i1)

A language can have distinct, though sometimes partially overlapping, sets of closed-class forms that represent the number, amount, or degree of a phenomenon that is respectively individuated, continuous in substance, or continuous in quality.

Thus, for the individuated referents of a plural count noun in English, the number of them from zero to the entirety of a set can be represented by closed-class forms like those in *No / few / some / many / most / all members were present*. A set containing three or more individuals is required by *no, some, most,* and *all*, while a set of four/five or more is required by *few* and *many*.

A set of exactly two individuals is required by *both*, *either*, and *neither*, as well as by the preposition *between* (*a basketball between the boulders*) and by the dual in nouns, while a set of two or more is required by the plural in nouns, and of three or more by the preposition *among* (*a basketball among the boulders*).

For the continuous substance represented by a mass noun, the amount of it can be represented by closed-class forms like those in *No / little / some / much / most / all water is polluted*. And for the continuously qualitative referent of an adjective, the degree of it can be represented by closed-class forms like those in *He is un- / somewhat / rather / quite / very friendly*.

4.1.9.2   Comparison of Quantities (D1i2)

Other closed-class forms represent the comparison of one quantity with one or more others. This is seen for the individuated referents of a plural count noun in *As for books, he has more/fewer than you; as many as you; the most/ least of anyone*. It is seen for the continuous referent of a mass noun in *As for money, he has more/less than you; as much as you; the most/least of anyone*. And it is seen for the continuous qualitative referent of an adjective in *He is friendlier than you; less friendly than you; as friendly as you; the friendliest/least friendly of all*.

Further, some closed-class forms represent a comparison with a fixed comparand. This comparand is semantically constrained—it can refer, perhaps solely, to necessity, desire, and expectation. Thus, *enough*, as in *I have enough food*, can be glossed as 'at least as much as needed'. *Too*, as in *I have too much food*, can be glossed as 'more than desired'. And, as seen [4.1.5], *only* as in *Only a hundred people came* can be glossed as 'less than expected'.

In addition, closed-class prefixes can be added to verb roots to represent an increase or decrease in amount, as in *up/ downsize*, or to indicate too much or not enough in degree, as in *over/underestimate*.

4.1.10   Ontology (D1j)

In the schematic system of ontology, the whole of a closed class is associated with a particular conceptual domain, and its members are associated with conceptual categories that subdivide the domain. The members classify the domain into an ontology.

For example, the closed class consisting of Wh- and yes/no forms is associated with the conceptual domain 'questioning'. Crosslinguistically, its members subdivide this domain into at least nine conceptual categories. Thus, *what* is prototypically associated with asking about the conceptual category of an 'inanimate entity'; *who*: a 'person'; *where*: a 'location'; *when*: a 'time'; *how*: a 'manner'; *why*: a 'reason'; Russian *skol'ko* ('how much/many'): a 'quantity'; Russian *kakoy* ('what kind of'): a 'quality'; and Yiddish *tsi* (*Tsi kumt er?* "Is he coming?"): 'polarity'. Together, these member-specified conceptual categories classify the conceptual domain of what can be asked about into an ontology.

Comparably, the closed class consisting of different lexical categories is associated with the conceptual domain 'type of referent', and its members are prototypically associated with the different types that together subdivide the domain into an ontology, as seen in (7).

(7) The lexical category before the colon is prototypically associated with the conceptual category after the colon.
 a. noun: 'entity'
 b. verb: 'process/state'
 c. adjective: 'attribute of an entity'
 d. adverb(ial marker): 'attribute of a process'
 e. preposition: 'relation of one entity to another'
 f. clause: 'event'
 g. sentence: 'proposition'
 h. subordinating conjunction: 'relation of one proposition to another'
 i. coordinating conjunction: 'relation between equipollent propositions'

In turn, each of the preceding lexical categories governs a closed class of different lexical subcategories associated with their own concepts that again form an ontology. Thus, the closed class of lexical subcategories under "noun" is associated with the conceptual subdomain 'type of entity', which its members further subdivide into a new ontology, as seen in (8).

(8) The nominal subcategories before the colon are prototypically associated with the conceptual categories after the colon.
 a. count / mass: 'bounded / unbounded'
 b. common / proper: 'nonunique / unique'
 c. uniplex / multiplex (e.g., cow / cattle): 'one / two or more'
 d. inalienable / alienable: 'autonomous / relational'
 e. masculine / feminine / neuter: 'male / female / without sexual differentiation'

Additional ontologies can be seen in the preceding subsections of [4.1]. They include the conceptual domain of spatial paths and sites subdivided by the meanings of the several score satellites and prepositions in English over a range containing 'forth' and 'among' [4.1.1 (D1a1)]; the conceptual domain of force dynamics, as subdivided by the dozen or so grammatical devices representing basic force-dynamic patterns as well as by the dozen or so English modals (T1 c8) [4.1.4]; the domain of communicative purpose, subdivided in English by the eight or so grammatical devices representing particular purposes ranging from 'informing' to 'rousing' [4.1.7]; and the conceptual domain of quantity, as subdivided in English by the half dozen or so count specifiers from 'no' to 'all' [4.1.9 (D1i1)].

4.2 Content Patterning (D2)

Another major mechanism by which language structures conceptual content might be called "content patterning". This consists of the patterns in which a language partitions and arranges what might otherwise be considered a conceptual continuum. Such patterns occur in the morpheme and the two arenas of its assembly, the lexicon (inventory) and the expression, discussed next in order.

4.2.1 In the Morpheme (D2a)

The mechanism of content patterning is first in effect in that every language bounds off portions of the conceptual continuum to form the individual meanings associated with its morphemes. This is the process of "lexicalizing" or "packaging".

The mechanism is further in effect in that the content within those portions is structured. the patterns of such structuring constitute "frame semantics" (Fillmore, 1976). The content of a morpheme can in the first instance be divided into a "core meaning" and an "associated meaning", addressed next in order.

4.2.1.1 Core Meaning (D2a1)

A morpheme's core meaning can—through procedures often called "componential analysis" or "unpacking"—be taken to include or consist of certain semantic components. These components can be either idiosyncratic or part of a pattern, where the pattern can in turn be either different from or the same as that in a familiar closed class—three types next illustrated in order.

Idiosyncratic Core Semantic Components. Idiosyncratic semantic components are seen in the core meaning of the verb *pry*, as in *I pried the board off the wall* (T6). The main semantic components are 1) the force comes from an object inserted and pivoted between the Figure and Ground; 2) The Figure resists; and 3) The Figure moves away gradually. Where each of these in turn is absent, the speaker might instead say respectively *I yanked / flipped / popped the board off the wall.*

Systematic Core Semantic Components Unlike Ones in a Closed Class. The second type of semantic component is seen for example in certain English sets of three nouns for animate species. In each set, the core meanings of all three nouns include the semantic component for a particular species, but that of one noun also includes the semantic component 'young' and another the semantic component 'castrated'. 'Young' is probably not, and 'castrated' is certainly not, in the meaning of any closed-class form. Yet these semantic components occur systematically across these open-class sets. With the noun for the species alone appearing first, examples of such sets are: *horse/foal/gelding; cow/calf/ox; sheep/lamb/wether; pig/piglet/barrow; chicken/chick/capon; person/child/eunuch*.[5]

Systematic Core Semantic Components like Ones in a Closed Class. The third type of semantic component is seen in these same sets. Each set has a noun whose core meaning also includes the semantic component 'male' and another with the semantic component 'female'. These are components also present in some languages' closed-class forms marking gender. Thus, the sets just listed also include *stallion, mare; cow, bull; ram, ewe; boar, sow; cock, hen; man, woman*.

Other examples of the third type are the semantic components 'uniplex' and 'multiplex' in the meanings of *cow* and *cattle*, and the semantic component 'negative' in the verb *fail*.

4.2.1.2   *Associated Meaning (D2a2)*
Within the total meaning of a morpheme, the associated meaning can itself be subdivided into at least five sectors (T15). This patterning holds for both open-class morphemes and closed-class morphemes, but only the former are illustrated here.

Holistic Sector. The "holistic sector" within a morpheme's associated meaning represents the conceptual whole that the morpheme's core meaning is necessarily a part of. Thus, the core meaning of the verb *buy* most directly represents a buyer's acquisition of certain merchandise. But the verb's holistic sector represents the whole commercial transaction—including the transfer of merchandise from the seller to the buyer and of a payment from the buyer to the seller—of which that acquisition is only a part.

Infrastructure Sector. The "infrastructure sector" is a conceptual underpinning that the core meaning presupposes but is not wholly determined by. Thus, the core meaning of the noun *heaven* most directly represents the concepts of a luminous space in the sky near God. But it rests on an infrastructure

---

5   Although *gelding* and *piglet* are actually bimorphemic in English, their German counterparts are monomorphemic.

of particular beliefs about divinity, soul, afterlife, goodness, and reward vs. punishment.

Collateral Sector. The "collateral sector" adds concepts commonly associated with the core meaning but incidental to it. Thus, the core meaning of the noun *bucket* represents a roughly cylindrical tapered foot-high and wide object with an open top spanned by a handle. And its collateral sector represents the commonly associated function of using the object to convey material placed in it. But that association is only ancillary, suspended when referring, say, to a gold bucket sitting on a pedestal as an art exhibit.

Disposition Sector. The "disposition sector" comprises the aspects of a morpheme's meaning that arise from its grammatical properties. Thus, the core meaning of the Spanish noun *puente* is the concept of an inanimate bridge. But its grammatical masculine gender can induce a penumbra of concepts of maleness in its disposition sector (Boroditsky et al., 2003).

Attitude Sector. And the "attitude sector" mainly consists of speaker attitudes pertaining to the morpheme's core meaning or its use. Thus, the core meaning of the adjective *paltry* is the concept 'small in amount'. But its attitude sector represents a disparaging attitude by the speaker toward that smallness.

4.2.2   In the Lexicon (D2b)

The mechanism of content patterning when at work in the lexicon is seen in the size of different morpheme classes, in the balance between closed- and open-class forms, and in the semantic relations among the extant morphemes, discussed next in order.

4.2.2.1   *Morpheme Class Size (D2b1)*

Across the lexicons of different languages, particular classes of morphemes, as defined by certain criteria, can vary greatly in size from prodigious to minimal. The pattern of certain large and small classes in a language often correlates with the presence of a particular productive closed-class construction that is also in the lexicon. The construction assembles the larger classes in an expression. This design can be seen, for example, by comparing a satellite-framed with a verb-framed language, here, respectively English and Spanish (T2 c3).

The English lexicon includes a prodigious number of colloquial Manner verbs, few colloquial Path verbs, and very many Path satellites and prepositions. It also includes a colloquial construction in which all the sizable ones of these categories of elements readily fit together. The main portion of this construction—Manner verb - Path satellite Path preposition—can be seen in *I ran out of the house*. The lexicon, however, lacks a colloquial construction that would string together a Path verb, a Manner-verb gerund, and a Path preposition, as in *I exited running from the house*, awkward at best.

By contrast, the Spanish lexicon includes comparatively fewer Manner verbs, a sizable number of colloquial Path verbs, almost no Path satellites, and a small number of Path prepositions. It also includes a colloquial construction—the one uncolloquial in English—that compatibly combines the more sizable ones of these categories, as seen in *Salí corriendo de la casa* which can be glossed much like the awkward English sentence above. Correlatively, it lacks the full colloquial English construction.[6]

4.2.2.2 Closed- and Open-Class Balance (D2b2)

If a closed class and an open class are syntactically associated in a language, then a type of concept expressed extensively by the closed class tends not to be so expressed by the open class, and vice versa. This is the pattern of "semantic unilocality" in which a type of concept tends to be expressed by only one of the constituents in a construction (T14).

For example, the presence in English of an extensive closed class of satellites and prepositions expressing Path seems to correlate with the fact that the open-class verbs associated with it express little Path. Thus, the Manner verb *dance* expresses essentially no path in its meaning and so is compatible with virtually the full range of path expressions, as seen in *The two of them danced into and then out of the room. / up the stairs. / out the door onto the veranda. / past the statuary. / through the crowd across the ballroom. / apart from each other.*

Complementarily, French has only a small closed class expressing Path while its open-class verbs express Path extensively, whether by itself or together with manner. Of the Path + Manner type, French for example has *grimper* 'climb up', *débouler* 'roll down a slope', *dériver* 'drift off from an expected course', and *arpenter* 'pace back and forth along the same straight bounded line'—a type of verb much rarer in English.

Semantic unilocality can also be in effect where the closed class at issue is used extensively but has just one or a few members. For example, the productive availability in English of the prefixes *un-/dis-/de-* expressing "reverse versality" (T14 s3.5)—as in *untie/disassemble/defund*—may correlate with a relative dearth of verb roots representing such reversal. But Mandarin, which lacks such a closed-class form, seemingly has more simplex verb roots expressing reversal, like *jiě* 'unknot' (e.g., a tied sack/braid), *chāi* 'disassemble' (e.g.,

---

6 However, Spanish does have a simpler form of the English construction for non-boundary-crossing paths.

a bookshelf) or 'unfasten' (e.g., a plaque on a wall), and *qù* 'remove' (e.g., a stain). And other actions that in English are conceptualized as reversals, like *unwind* (wire from a spool) and *unroll* (cloth from a bolt), are reconceptualized in Mandarin as "proverse" actions by constructions glossable respectively as "pull straight" and "pull flat" (Jian-Sheng Guo, p.c.).

4.2.2.3 *Cross-Morpheme Relations (D2b3)*
The meanings represented by the morphemes present in a language's lexicon can in turn bear certain semantic relations to each other. Certain of these relations fall under the category of "hierarchy". Four specific hierarchies—indicated by the subordinate level first and the superordinate second (T15 s2)—are hyponym-hypernym (e.g., dog-mammal), part-whole (e.g., petal-flower), member-category (e.g., Chicago-city), and analytic-synthetic (e.g., two-pair).

Still further relations are synonymy—various forms with a roughly single meaning—and polysemy—a single form with various meanings. In the case of polysemy, content patterning is again evident in the arrangement formed by the various meanings. By radial category theory (Brugmann and Lakoff, 1988), this arrangement is one in which one of the meanings is basic and the remaining meanings differ from it and from each other by conceptual increments that largely have a structuring function across languages.

4.2.3 In Expression (D2c)
Where a larger conceptual whole is represented by a portion of discourse, the mechanism of content patterning is in play where the whole can be parceled out in different arrangements within that portion (T2 c4 s2).

We can illustrate first with a crosslinguistic pattern difference over the scope of a sentence. Thus, where the conceptual whole is an agentive Motion situation, English characteristically expresses the Agent in the subject nominal, the coevent + Motion in the verb, the Figure in a direct object nominal, the Path in a satellite + preposition, and the Ground in an oblique nominal, as seen in *You tracked mud into my house*.

But Atsugewi places the Figure + Motion in the verb root, a causal coevent in a prefix, the Path + Ground in a suffix, and the pronominal Agent in inflections. This pattern occurs in the polysynthetic word /m-'-w-ma-st'aq̓-ipsn^{u}ik·-a/, which can function as a sentence referring to the same whole situation as the English example. In this word, an inflectional suffix (m-) expresses the Agent 'you'; a closed-class prefix (ma-) expresses the causal coevent 'by acting on the Figure with the feet'; a verb root (-st'aq̓-) expresses the Figure + Motion concept 'for runny icky material to move or be located'; a closed-class suffix (-ipsn^u)

expresses the Path + Ground concept 'into a volumetric enclosure'; and a closed-class suffix (-ik·) expresses the deictic concept 'hither'. The semantic pattern of this word might be rendered more closely in English as: You caused runny icky material (mud) to move hither into a volumetric enclosure (the house) by acting on it with your feet. The English and Atsugewi representations of the same conceptual complex can thus be seen to arrange its content in quite different patterns.

The same phenomenon occurs within a single language. For example, a speaker can arrange elements of a larger conceptual complex in different patterns over a discourse. Thus, a speaker can recount the events of an adventure iconically in their original order or in a range of different orders, each with its own semantic effect on the hearer (T2 c6). Or again, a speaker can select and sequence elements of a larger conceptual complex within a narrative so as to induce such particular cognitive effects in a hearer as surprise or suspense. A speaker's content manipulation of this kind can augment the communicative purposes represented by closed-class forms [4.1.7].

4.3 Content Selection (D3)

The remaining four major mechanisms for structuring conceptual content in language operate in concert to a great extent but, as feasible, are presented separately to highlight the characteristics of each. The present mechanism, then, "content selection", involves the speaker in the arena of expression. It is how the speaker "frames" her utterance(s). Specifically, given that she has a particular conceptual complex in mind to convey, it is largely her choice between whether to include or exclude the representation of certain content in that complex and, if included, the choice among alternative representations of it. We discuss these two types of choice next in order, and then constraints on choice.

4.3.1 Inclusion vs. Omission (D3a)

In her production process, a speaker generally first has a conceptual complex that she wants the hearer to experience, and then selects enough of that complex for explicit representation so that he can infer the remainder. What the hearer infers thus complements the portion of the conceptual complex overtly included by the speaker and fully or approximately captures the omitted portion. The included concepts represented explicitly are generally more salient and belong to the area of semantics, while the omitted concepts to be inferred are less salient and belong to pragmatics [1.3].

Both the speaker and the hearer processes are presented here together due to their close correlation—though, in this taxonomy, the hearer's inference is also listed without further discussion as D4 in [4.4]. The role of context in the speaker's selections and the hearer's interpretation of an utterance is discussed separately in [4.5].

Speaker omissions of different scopes can be considered and they are presented next roughly from smaller to larger. Correlatively, the hearer's process of inference generally proceeds from more to less constrained.

4.3.1.1   Ellipsis (D3a1)

Ellipsis can be divided into two types here called "copy ellipsis" and "shortlist ellipsis". In copy ellipsis, the speaker omits the smallest amount of explicit content within a sentence under strict syntactic conditions and the hearer is to copy concepts already expressed overtly elsewhere in the current or preceding sentence to fill in the omission. This covers most of the types of ellipsis addressed in the literature, such as gapping, stripping, sluicing, comparative deletion, and answer fragments. For example, gapping is seen in *Wes likes wine with dinner and his wife [likes] beer [with dinner]*, where the hearer copies earlier concepts to fill in the brackets.

In shortlist ellipsis, the concept supplied by the hearer is not represented in the surrounding material but is one of a small set of alternatives, determined by the context—hence, still under much constraint but less than above (T12 s3.4). This pattern is seen in *Rice is easy [for one/me/us/you/him/her/them] to digest*. It is seen in *Can I have some [of this/that]?*, as said to someone standing nearby holding a pitcher of lemonade. And it is seen in *The bus stop you want is across the street [from here/there]*.

The limiting case of shortlist ellipsis, where only one option is available to the hearer, can occur in a divergence from an otherwise fixed pattern. To illustrate, the modal-request construction [5.3] semantically requires the second person hearer as subject. Overtly, though, the third person can appear instead, as in *Could your kids please turn their music down?*. Here, the hearer inserts the concept of the second person's influence over the third person, as if the speaker had said *Could you please ask/tell your kids to turn their music down?*.

4.3.1.2   Omission in Windowing (D3a2)

A generally larger and less constrained portion of conceptual content can be omitted from explicit representation in a sentence in the process of "windowing" (T1 c4). This process can act where a sentence refers to a conceptually bounded "event frame" such as a bounded path, causal sequence, or turn of a cycle. Thus, for a bounded path, a speaker might express the whole of it, as in *The crate fell out of the plane through the air into the ocean*. Or she could omit one or two of the path's beginning, middle, or terminal portions. Thus, she could omit the middle, as in *The crate fell out of the plane into the ocean* or the middle and end as in *The crate fell out of the plane*. The hearer will restore the missing conceptual portions largely on the basis of his general knowledge—here, under respectively more and less constraint.

Or, for a cycle, if a speaker says *The pen kept rolling off the desk*, the hearer will likely add in the concept 'and I kept replacing it'.

4.3.1.3   *Intersentential Omission (D3a3)*
A speaker often omits a substantial amount of conceptual content between neighboring sentences, and the hearer, generally under less constraint than before, can infer it largely through general knowledge. For example, a host might say to a guest *Would you like some music on? I have to go put my daughter to sleep*. The hearer here is constrained by the conceptions expressed by the two sentences, but might infer that the conceptual content connecting them resembles what would be expressed if the speaker had inserted something like *I ask because you might like the entertainment that music can provide to compensate for your remaining alone without my company, since I will be gone for a while due to the unavoidable fact that ....*

4.3.1.4   *Extrasentential Omission (D3a4)*
The greatest amount of conceptual content generally unspecified in an utterance consists of what is taken for granted in our physical, psychological, and societal knowledge of the world—that is, notions at large in the culture whose validity generally does not come under our conscious consideration. It would in fact be all but impossible to specify the entirety of such knowledge. Every utterance is thus conceptually abstractive(T6).

We can illustrate such omission first just for physical knowledge close to the conceptual scope of a sentence. Thus, a speaker saying *I put the glass of water down* would generally not specify the concepts that the glass was upright, not upside down; a few inches across, not three feet wide; gripped by my hand during its descent, not by a mechanical device; and at the end supported on a clear horizontal surface, not balanced on a wire. The hearer will supply all these unspecified concepts in his conceptualization of the utterance's total meaning.

And we can illustrate a broader scope of omission with the classic example of a guest saying to a host: *It's a bit chilly in here*. Within the content omitted by the speaker, the more immediately pertinent aspects of general knowledge include such physical concepts as that, in cold weather, cold air can enter an enclosure through an aperture; such psychological concepts as that a person can feel uncomfortable from contact with cold air; and such socio-cultural concepts as that, typically, a guest does not act directly on the host's property and a host aims for the guest's comfort. The hearer infers all this from the utterance and, from its context, infers that it is not a simple assertion of opinion but an indirect request for him to close the window.

4.3.2 Alternatives of Inclusion (D3b)

Where a speaker has selected a certain portion of a conceptual complex for explicit representation in an utterance, she can further select among alternatives for such representation. This is her cognitive capacity for "conceptual alternativity" (T1 c3). The speaker here selects among different "construals" (Langacker, 1993), "perspectives" (Clark, 1997), or "conceptualizations" (T1 c1) of that portion of content. Such alternatives can occur on a smaller or larger scale.

Within the smaller scope of a single sentence, there are innumerably different categories of alternative choice, several of which are selected here to illustrate the range. In the category of spatial frames, a speaker opting to include reference to the spatial relation between a particular Figure and Ground—say, a bike and church—can select any of the alternatives in *The bike was behind/west of/left of the church* to represent respectively a Ground-based, field-based, and observer-based frame (T1 c3). Or for the category of reality status [4.1.6], a speaker might say either *I regret that I didn't see the film* or *I wish I had seen the film* to foreground either a factual or a counterfactual stance on the same situation (T1 c4 s7.2).

Or again, a speaker choosing to represent a subject's affect can select between representing inner state or outer behavior, as in saying either *He was happy/afraid/cold* or *He was smiling/trembling/shivering*. And a speaker choosing to express the concept 'very small' can lexically represent it together with any of a range of attitudes, such as that of amazement over the degree in *tiny*, scorn in *puny*, endearedness toward a child in *itsy-bitsy*, sarcasm in *teensy-weensy*, and seriousness in *minuscule* (T15 s6.5.2).

In addition to conceptual categories, the alternatives available within a sentence can range along innumerable parameters. Thus, a speaker choosing to represent a subject's Manner of motion can select along a parameter of its degree of specificity by saying *She went/walked/limped to the party*. Or where a hearer had heard the name "Chris" and mistakenly asked "Who is he?", a speaker might correct his gender choice with different degrees of elaboration from slight to great, as by saying *She's my boss* or *!-SHE's my boss*, or *It's a "she", not a "he": she's my boss*.

On a larger scale, a speaker can, for example, choose different styles in which to present the same conceptual content over a discourse. She might present it, say, earnestly, humorously, or melodramatically.

4.3.3   Constraints on Selection (D3c)

The mechanism of content selection includes not only affordances, the focus so far, but also constraints.

4.3.3.1   *Constraints on Inclusion and Omission (D3c1)*

The speaker is constrained regarding what to include—both obligatory inclusions and omissions. An example of obligatory inclusion is the requirement in English that a count noun indicate whether its referent is singular or plural—a speaker wanting to use the noun cannot choose to omit the conceptual category of number.

An example of obligatory omission is a "blocked argument" (T15). For instance, though the argument structure of the verb *buy* readily permits mention of the seller, as in *I bought a book for $50 from a clerk today*, the verb *spend* blocks explicit reference to the seller, though one is implicitly present, as seen in *I spent $50 for a book *from/by/with/to/at a clerk today*. A speaker wanting to include reference to the seller must use means other than a simple preposition.

Slobin's (e.g., 1996) principle of "thinking for speaking" addresses the attention that a speaker must direct to those aspects of a situation that require linguistic representation. But an extension of this principle to "not thinking for not speaking" might be proposed where a blocked or simply absent linguistic representation of a particular situational aspect results in disattention to that aspect.

4.3.3.2   *Constraints on Alternatives of Inclusion (D3c2)*

A speaker is also constrained regarding the alternatives to select among. For example, she is limited to the constructions available in her language for a given semantic domain. Thus, in the domain of referent prominence, a speaker of English, with its stronger constraints on constituent order, cannot select among the extensive constituent-order possibilities available to a Yiddish speaker to express subtly different patterns of emphasis. In that language, for example, the perhaps most unmarked constituent order for "He ate the apple there quite fast" is *Er hot dortn gegesn dem epl gants shnel* 'he has there eaten the apple quite fast'. But a speaker can achieve diverse effects by moving *gegesn, dortn, dem epl* or *gants shnel* either singly or in certain combinations) to the beginning of the sentence (thereby triggering subject-auxiliary inversion) or by shifting their locations within the sentence. If comparable effects are to be achieved in English, the speaker must draw on means other than constituent order, such as lexical choice, stress, and construction type (T2 c6).

4.4 *Content Inference (D4)*

This fourth major mechanism for structuring content in language, "content inference", involves the hearer in the arena of expression. By it, a hearer infers the portion of the conceptual content that the speaker had intended him to become aware of but had omitted from explicit representation. This speaker process of omission was discussed in [4.3.1], and the hearer process, which complements it, was treated there as well and so is not further discussed here.

4.5 *Context (D5)*

A fifth major mechanism by which language structures conceptual content is the use of context. This mechanism specifically pertains to language's built-in *reliance* on context for certain structuring functions that it accordingly need not mark explicitly.

For one characterization of it, context includes everything that can affect an utterance's framing by a speaker or interpretation by a hearer. More specifically, context outside an utterance proper can include personal, cognitive, and social dimensions of its speaker and hearer, such as their gender, status, common ground, and general knowledge; its spatial and temporal location; its physical surrounding; the societally defined category of its circumstances; and the thematic character of the discourse it is embedded in. Two further forms of context lie within the scope of an utterance. For any morpheme within an utterance, the remaining morphemes are context for it. And an utterance's modality—whether it is, say, spoken, signed, or written—can be considered part of its context. Citing these specific forms of it, we next discuss context under three headers based on speaker and/or hearer use of it.

4.5.1 Context for Speaker Omission and Hearer Inference (D5a)

In each example of [4.3.1], the use of context enabled the omission of content by the speaker and the inference of it by the hearer. Several of these are repeated and discussed next, organized by the type of context used.

The type of utterance-internal context that consists of the morphemes present in the utterance enabled the speaker to omit and the hearer to infer the gapped content in *Wes likes wine with dinner and his wife beer*. Specifically here, the constituents *likes* and *with dinner* already occurring in the earlier clause were tapped for a second application in the later clause.

The type of context that consists of the thematic character of the discourse containing an utterance was in play in the sentence *Rice is easy to digest*. If the theme had been about different kinds of foods, the likely concept was 'for one', referring to a generic eater. But if the theme was the speaker's health, the likelihood was that she had omitted and the hearer had inferred the concept 'for me', referring back to herself.

Or again, the type of context consisting of the utterance's physical surroundings would have been in play in the lemonade requester's saying *Can I have some?*, where the speaker was able to omit and the hearer to infer the concept 'of this' or 'of that' in accord with the pitcher's distance from the speaker.

And another type of context consists of the speaker's and hearer's general knowledge. Knowledge about the physical world enabled the speaker to omit and the hearer to infer the middle portion—the concept 'through the air'—of the bounded path depicted in *The crate fell out of the plane into the ocean*.

And knowledge about the social world was in play in the example where a host says to her guest *Would you like some music on? I have to go put my daughter to sleep*. It enabled the speaker to omit spelling out the connection between her offer of music and her need to attend to her daughter—and for the hearer to infer the connection.

A further type of context not illustrated above is the interlocutors' "common ground" (Clark and Brennan, 1991), which includes the concepts that the speaker and hearer know they hold jointly, largely due to their history together. Thus, a speaker who was earlier told by a friend that he planned to go to a movie can later begin a discourse with the friend by saying simply *What did you see*, without further specifying time or category, and the friend will infer the event intended.

4.5.2   Context for Speaker Selection among Alternatives (D5b)

The speaker's use of context was just addressed for her selection of what to omit and is now addressed for her selection among alternatives for inclusion. The new examples here also illustrate still further types of context.

Thus, a speaker can select among different registers for expressing the same conceptual content based on certain personal dimensions of the hearer, as where she addresses either a toddler by saying *Gramma's going bye-bye* or an adult by saying *Your grandmother's leaving now*.

And the same conceptual content can be represented differently in accord with the societally defined circumstance of its expression. Thus, the sentence *Would you like to sit down?* might be produced in a coffee house; *Please take a seat* in a lawyer's office; and *I pray you be seated* in a medievally set fantasy novel.

4.5.3 Context for Other Hearer Interpretation (D5c)

In the preceding two subsections, context was discussed for its use in both kinds of speaker framing—inclusion/ omission and alternative choice—as well as in one kind of hearer interpretation, his inference of omitted content. We here address its use in other kinds of hearer interpretation, namely, in picking the relevant sense from a polysemous range, in determining the target of a trigger (i.e., a deictic or anaphor), and in resolving an ambiguity. Again, a range of context types helps these processes.

4.5.3.1 *Selecting a Polysemous Sense (D5c1)*

One major task for a hearer is to select the relevant sense from a morpheme's polysemous or homophonous range, and one kind of context abetting this task is utterance-internal—the morpheme's neighbors. Thus, if a speaker says *I checked the market figures—my stock is down*, the morphemes in the expression form each other's context. They lead the hearer to select the 'ascertain' sense of *check*, the 'financial exchange' sense of *market*, the 'number' sense of *figure*, the 'financial instrument' sense of *stock*, and the 'reduced' sense of *down* (T6 s2.3.2).

Another type of context abetting this task of polysemy selection is a discourse's overall theme. Thus, a discussion of cooking will lead a hearer to select the 'soup base' sense of *stock* instead of, say, its 'financial instrument' sense of the preceding example.

4.5.3.2 *Determining a Target (D5c2)*

The type of context consisting of the perceivable physical surroundings can help a hearer determine the target of a deictic [1.4]. Thus, if a speaker atop a hill points down toward a lagoon and says *Mist forms there in the morning*, the lagoon's having an outer perimeter as a perceivable element of environmental structure helps the hearer settle on the whole surface of the water as the target of *there* rather than the single point that the speaker gestures at (T12 s9.2.1).

4.5.3.3 *Resolving an Ambiguity (D5c3)*

Several types of context in concert can help a hearer resolve ambiguities. For example, consider a speaker saying *I got snowed under in my work and had to come up for air*. The hearer will decide against the more basic meaning of *snowed under* as 'buried under snow' and of *come up for air* as 'swim to the surface of a body of water'. He will instead opt for their more idiomatic senses respectively of 'overwhelmed' and of 'take some respite'.

This choice may be based on four forms of context. First, the utterance-internal type of context from the presence of the phrase *in my work* militates against the concepts of snow or water. Second, a type of context consisting of conceptual coherence makes it implausible to combine being buried under snow and swimming through water. Third, the thematic topic type of context may inform the hearer that the discussion had been about projects, not about last winter's weather or diving. And fourth, the common ground type of context may inform the hearer that the speaker's life circumstances exclude any likelihood of snow burial or underwater activity.

4.6   *Interaction (D6)*
A sixth mechanism by which language structures conceptual content is interaction among the interlocutors of a speech event. Such interaction can consist of their taking each other's needs and actions into consideration, or the alternation of their roles as speaker and hearer—two possibilities addressed next in order.

4.6.1   Cross-Consideration (D6a)
A speaker and hearer cannot simply undertake their respective processes of production and interpretation independently, heedless of each other's constraints and requirements, but rather must take these into consideration for a speech event to succeed as a communication. In particular, the speaker must function as a proactive agent ensuring that her framing (i.e., what she includes explicitly and how she phrases that) and the available forms of context are adequate for the hearer to reconstruct the conceptual complex she wanted him to experience. In turn, the hearer must maintain a model of such endeavors by the speaker to guide him in determining the relevant context and concepts.

This mechanism of cooperation was not foregrounded during the discussion of speaker-hearer complementation above [4.3.1 and 4.5.1] but can be retroactively considered as an addition to it. For a fresh example here, a speaker needs to ensure cue adequacy in an act of targeting (T12 s1.5.1). Thus, a birder in thick woods who points and says *That's a whippoorwill* to a novice some meters away must ensure that he is at or can move to a location from which he can see her finger (gestural cue) and the bird (targetive cue); that he can act fast enough so that the bird is still there when he looks (chronal cue); and that he knows to peer up deep into the branches to spot the bird (epistemic and environmental cues). The hearer in turn must recognize these speaker's aims for cue adequacy in order to act quickly in spotting her gesture and following it to search visually through the branches for the target.

Such cooperation is also seen in Gricean maxims (Grice, 1975). Though these maxims are largely cast in terms of how the speaker should frame her utterance, their characterization as cooperative conversational principles also indicates that much of what guides the speaker is her understanding of the hearer's cognition. Thus, the maxim of quantity—basically, that a speaker's utterance should provide neither too little nor too much information—mainly depends on the needs of the hearer, not of the speaker. And the maxim of relevance can as readily concern what is relevant to the hearer as to the speaker.

4.6.2 Turn Taking (D6b)

Another type of interaction is turn taking, where an utterance by one interlocutor can provide the basis for a response from a second interlocutor, which can in turn occasion a further response from the first, and so on. There are specific sequences of such alternations in which each turn consists of a particular type of utterance (T12 s13.1). Sequences from two to five turns in length are discussed next in order.

There is a partial overlap between the phenomena covered here and earlier under "communicative purpose" [4.1.7]. The differences, though, are that earlier the communicative purpose had to be marked grammatically, which is not necessary here, and that a response was not in every case forthcoming from the initial addressee, which it is here.

4.6.2.1   Two-Turn Sequence (D6b1)

Frequent two-turn sequences—the "adjacency pairs" of conversation analysis (Schegloff and Sacks, 1973)—include a question and an answer (X: *Where are you?* Y: *In the kitchen*); a statement and a same-theme augment (X: *I didn't sleep much last night.* Y: *Yeah, I got up early myself*); a misstatement and a correction (X: *She is green-eyed.* Y: *No, she has !-blue eyes.*); an offer and an acceptance or refusal (X: *Have some chocolate.* Y: *Okay, I will.*); and a degreeting and its reciprocation (X: *Bye now.* Y: *See you later.*). Content is structured here in that the initial speaker's utterance provides a conceptual template with certain conditions for a complementary response, which the addressee then fulfills.

4.6.2.2   Three-Turn Sequence (D6b2)

An interaction sequence can also consist of three alternating turns. Thus, the "follow-up question sequence" consists of a statement, a question about some of its particulars, and an answer, as in: X: *The game is over.* Y: *Who won?* X: *The Warriors.*

Another three-turn sequence is a "Wh-echo-question" repair. Here, X makes a statement; Y did not clearly hear one constituent there and, to request its reutterance, uses a heightened-stressed Wh-word in its place along with sustained high pitch over the whole expression; and X repeats the unclear constituent with heightened stress—as in: X: *Macpherson totaled his car.* Y: *!-Who totaled his car?* X: *!-Macpherson did.*

4.6.2.3   *Four-Turn Sequence (D6b3)*
Four-turn sequences occur as well, for example, the sequence whose turns in succession represent the illocutionary effects of assertion, opposition, insistence, and concession (T12 s13.1.2). It is seen in: X: *I'm going to the store for cigarettes.* Y: *Please don't go—I need you here to get ready for the guests.* X: *Well, I'm going anyway.* Y: *So !-go then.* Here, each turn could end the sequence. Thus, the second utterance could end a two-turn "opposition sequence", the third utterance could end a three-turn "insistence sequence", and the fourth utterance could end a four-turn "concession sequence". Each illocutionary effect intrinsically occurs at the turn indicated and the last case is the one that exemplifies the four-turn sequence.

4.6.2.4   *Five-Turn Sequence (D6b4)*
The possibly longest sequence might be called the five-turn "exasperation sequence". It begins with the same three turns as in the Wh-echo-question sequence seen above. The fourth turn is then the "redoubled Wh-echo question construction" in which Y asks again about the still unclear constituent, now using doubly heightened stress on the Wh-word, as in: Y: *!!-Who totaled his car?*. And in the fifth turn, the original speaker repeats the unclear word now with doubly heightened stress on it and at times also with an intonation pattern suggesting exasperation in what could be called the "redoubled Wh- echo answer construction", as in X: *!!-Macpherson totaled his car.* This last construction is thus lexicalized to appear as the fifth turn in the five-turn exasperation sequence.

5   Combination (E)

A foundational design feature of language is that it is richly "combinatorial"—in every system at every level, smaller units combine to form larger units in accord with rules (T13). Where the units are semantic, such combination is ipso facto a means by which language structures conceptual content (and might have been included as a further mechanism under [4] but is presented here as a separate category in part due to its extensiveness).

Perhaps the main parameter along which the combination of semantic units varies is their type of relationship—additive, operational, idiomatic, or constructively discrepant—types treated next in order. Additional parameters involve whether the units combine cooccurrently or sequentially; whether they combine as a simple aggregate or in a structured pattern; and whether their combinations are preestablished in the language in a closed inventory or can be generated open-endedly by the speaker in an expression.

5.1   Additive (E1)

In the first type of combination, the values of the combining units add together without interfering with each other. This relationship can be seen within a hierarchy, across language divisions, in contraction and suppletion, in conflation, and in nesting, addressed next in order.

5.1.1   Within a Hierarchy (E1a)

The combination of units can form a hierarchy—here depicted as progressing upwards—in which smaller units combine to form larger units at a particular level, and these in turn can function as the smaller units that combine to form still larger units at the next higher level. At each such level, the combination is not fully free but accords with certain "rules", that is, with a particular set of affordances and constraints. The units relate to each other in terms of their places within the hierarchical structure. But they are additive in that the total effect consists of the accumulation of their values within those relationships, and in that the units do not interfere with each other, each manifesting its value independently of the others.

Units of form can comprise this type of hierarchy as readily as those of meaning, and their hierarchy is addressed first because the hierarchy of meaning units largely conforms to it.

5.1.1.1   The Form Hierarchy (E1a1)

What might be called the "main sequence" for form begins in any language with a closed inventory of phonetic distinctive features. These features can combine cooccurrently into phonemes in accord with rules of feature cooccurrence restrictions. Those phonemes that are licensed by the language then themselves form a second closed inventory, the phonemic inventory. In turn, these phonemes can combine sequentially into morphemic shapes (with the potential of cooccurrent stress or tone) in accord with rules of phonotactics. Those morphemic shapes that the language licenses then themselves form a third closed inventory, the lexicon of morphemic shapes. These morphemic shapes provide the form component of complete morphemes, as addressed in [5.1.2]. To this point in the main sequence, all the elements of form belong to closed inventories and are preestablished in the language. Forms at higher levels are generated by the speaker in expression.

Continuing the main sequence, in some languages, certain morphemes in the inventory can next combine sequentially into multimorphemic words in accord with rules of morphology. In turn, morphemes and multimorphemic words (if present) can combine sequentially and open-endedly into sentences in accord with rules of syntax. Such sentences can in turn be combined sequentially and open-endedly into a single-speaker turn, partly in accord with rules of information structure. Such individual-speaker turns can then combine into a dialog in accord with rules of turn taking.

In any dialog, all these levels of form coexist additively without interfering with each other.

5.1.1.2   *The Meaning Hierarchy (E1a2)*
Semantic combination largely tracks this formal main sequence, beginning at the level of the segmental morphemic shape where meaning first enters. For each such morphemic shape, semantic components can combine cooccurrently to yield a morphemic meaning in accord with rules of conceptual compatibility.

The combination can be either in a simple aggregation or in a structured pattern. Exemplifying an aggregation, the meaning of the morphemic shape *these* (as in *My wife likes these*—accompanied by a gesture) has the semantic components 'proximal', 'multiplex', 'entity-like' (not, say, locative), 'nonsentient', 'third-person', and 'deictic' (T12 c2). Exemplifying a structured pattern, the meaning of the morphemic shape *across* (as in *The board lay across the road*) has semantic components arrayed to form a particular geometric schema (T4). All such combinations of semantic components within a language form a closed inventory—the lexicon of morphemic meanings—which is larger than that for morphemic shapes due to polysemy.

Semantic combination next occurs across the morphemes of a multimorphemic word, where the meanings of the morphemes are added in some sequence rather than concurrently. The combination can again be a simple aggregation, as in *walked*, where the gait and tense concepts simply compound, or it can exhibit a structured pattern. A simpler example of the latter is seen in *juggler*, where the meaning of the suffix *-er* might be represented as 'person who __s', requiring that the meaning of the verb occur at the locus of the blank. A more complex pattern is seen in *untestedness*, where the meaning of the whole word can be built up by adding the meanings of the morphemes in the sequence *test, -ed, un-, -ness*.

Above the level of the word, all additive semantic combinations are sequential, generated by the speaker in the arena of expression, and open-ended. Thus, at the sentence level in *The young woman walked up to the juggler in the plaza to ask for lessons*, the meanings of the mono- and multimorphemic words that compose it do not simply aggregate but combine in accord with the rules of compositionality, which follow the branched hierarchical patterns of the sentence's phrase structure (with special provision for discontinuous constituents where they occur). For example, the concept associated with the morpheme *young* combines in the first instance with that associated with *woman* in an attribute-substrate relation—rather than with the concept associated with, say, *plaza*. And this higher-level conceptual combination, together with the semantic contribution from *the*, combines in the next instance with the concept associated with the verb phrase in an Agent-action relation—and not, say, with the concept associated with the verb *juggle*.

The meanings of such sentences can in turn combine to form the meaning of a single speaker's turn in accord with rules of coherence/cohesion. And the meanings of such turns can in turn combine into the meaning of an interlocutor dialog in accord with, among other rules, Gricean maxims.

As in the form hierarchy, all the cited semantic elements combine additively without interfering with each other, whether within a level or across levels.

5.1.2 Across Language Divisions (E1b)

A morpheme—that is, a minimal concept-associated linguistic construct [1.2]—generally constitutes a combination of elements from all three major divisions of language: form, grammar, and meaning [1]. In any given language, all such cross-division combinations together constitute its lexicon of morphemes. This three-part association thus amplifies Saussure's (1959) two-part association between form and meaning.[7]

To take a particular morpheme for illustration, its form (morphemic shape) consists of the phonemic sequence /mʌðəɹ/. This form combines with the meaning 'woman who has borne a child'. The form also combines with a particular grammatical complex consisting of the constituent status "open class"; the lexical category "noun"; the subcategories "count", "common", "uniplex",

---

7   Some closed-class morphemes do combine only two language divisions. Thus, Latin stem vowels, which mark a verb's conjugation, combine form and grammar without meaning. And the combination of grammar and meaning without form can be exemplified by the association between the lexical noun subcategory "proper" and the meaning 'unique'.

"relational"; and requirements for the anaphor *she* and the relative pronoun *who* (rather than which).

This triune combination is additive because the three language divisions contribute their own values without interfering with each other. Each of them could in principle vary independently of the others without reducing the potential viability of the combination as a morpheme. This "arbitrariness" of the form's relation to the meaning is the property that identifies the form as a "symbol" of the meaning (e.g., Peirce, 1955). However, the form's comparably arbitrary relation to the grammar is a largely unrecognized fact without a standard term to designate it.

But this proposed arbitrariness needs several hedges. One is that morphemic shapes associated with closed-class semantic categories tend to be shorter than those for open-class ones. Another is that some morphemic shapes are semantically constrained—for example, heightened stress readily combines with a concept of 'correction' but would be less likely to combine with one of, say, 'dog'. And a third is onomatopoeia or sound symbolism—a type of iconicity—where a morpheme's sound is taken to resemble its meaning, as in the reference of *caw* to a crow's call.

5.1.3   In Contraction/Suppletion (E1c)

A contraction and a suppletive form (of one type) are alike in that both consist of a single segmental form that represents the combined semantics of what would otherwise be two or more adjacent morphemes. They might be replaceable by such separate forms or occur in a paradigm some of whose other entries still consist of separate forms. Both cases are additive—the single form adds together the meanings of the represented forms and their grammatical relationship.

One difference between the two is that, in a contraction, some phonemes of the represented morphemes are still present whereas, in suppletion, the form is phonologically unrelated to them. Another difference is that the represented forms in general are free in contraction and bound in suppletion.

In English, an example of contraction is *won't* representing *will not*—/wont/ for /wɪl nat/. An example of suppletion is *worse* representing *bad* plus the comparative suffix *-er*.

5.1.4   In Conflation (E1d)

Seemingly every language can represent certain complex event structures either more analytically or more synthetically. Such a complex structure consists of one event in a certain semantic relation with another event. The analytic representation then consists of one clause in a corresponding syntactic relation with another clause. But the synthetic representation consists of a single clause, one in which the two analytic clauses and their relation are "conflated". Such a single clause thus represents all the components of a multi-event structure combined additively. It in effect represents the original structure as if it were a new single complex event—what (T2 c3) calls a "macro-event".

Some complex event structures—for example, a conditional (*I'll go to a movie if I eat soon*)—seem never to have single-clause representation. But others frequently do. One such is a "Manner" structure in which, to simplify, one component is a motion event X consisting of a Figure moving with respect to a Ground, a second component is an activity event Y in which the Figure exhibits a certain action, and the third component is a relation in which event Y functions as the Manner in which the Figure moves in event X. To illustrate, event X could be that of a top moving into the kitchen and event Y that of the top spinning. English could represent this structure analytically with two clauses, as in *The top went into the kitchen, spinning the while*, or synthetically in the single clause: *The top spun into the kitchen.*

Another complex event structure often represented synthetically involves agentive causation. To specify one type, event X is a Manner structure like that just described, event Y consists of a volitional Agent acting physically on the Figure of event X, and the relation of event Y to event X is that of causation—event X takes place because of event Y. English can again represent this structure more analytically as in *The top spun into the kitchen because I acted on the top* or more synthetically as in the single clause: *I spun the top into the kitchen.*

5.1.5   In Nesting (E1e)

Multiple instances of the same conceptual category can be combined within a single sentence to represent a nesting pattern in which each level does not interfere conceptually with the others. Such a pattern can be represented by a mix of both closed- and open-class forms.

To illustrate first with temporal configuration, an initial level of a single semelfactive occurrence is expressed by *The beacon flashed* (*as I looked over*). A second level in which such a single occurrence is iterated appears in *The beacon kept flashing*. A third level in which such an iteration is bounded appears in *The beacon flashed five times in a row*. A fourth level in which such a bounded sequence is itself iterated appears in *The beacon kept flashing five times at a stretch*. And a fifth level in which this iteration is itself bounded appears in *The beacon flashed five times at a stretch for three hours*. This five-level nested pattern is schematized in (9), where a dot represents a flash (T1 c1).

(9) [!!!!!] - [!!!!!] .... [!!!!!] - [!!!!!]

Similarly, five levels of spatial configuration are nested in *I saw three ponds full of groups of five ducks each*. In fact, this nesting has exactly the same pattern represented in (9), but with the dots now representing ducks (T1 c1).

Further, five levels of temporal perspective are nested in *At the punchbowl, I was about to meet my first wife-to-be*. This sentence places a viewpoint at time t1 that prospectively pictures a subsequent encounter with a woman at t2, a subsequent marriage to her at t3, a subsequent marriage to another woman at t4, and places another viewpoint at the present time t5 that retrospectively pictures all the foregoing (T1 c1).

Additionally, six levels from the schematic system of quantity are nested in *I've had so very much too many more misfortunes than him*. And in *The lion caught up with the deer*, one motion event in which the lion as Figure moves to the location of the deer as Ground is nested within another motion event in which the lion and deer together as a compound Figure move across the terrain as Ground.

5.2   *Operational (E2)*

A second major type of combination is in the arena of expression. In it, the meanings of two morphemes in a construction are not statically additive—rather, one of them dynamically operates on the other. Such an "operational" morpheme is lexicalized to alter a component of the other morpheme's meaning—it initiates an operation which shifts that component from one specific value to another along a particular parameter.

A morpheme with this operational type of combination can be bound or free, closed- or open-class. A bound closed-class example is the verb prefix *un-*, as in *untie* [4.2.2]. It shifts the semantic component 'proverse' in the original verb to 'retroverse' along a parameter of "versality" (T14 s3.5).

A free closed-class example is *almost* which, when combining with an accomplishment verb as in *My leg almost healed*, operates on the aspectual component of the verb. When unaltered, the aspect of accomplishment indicates that some process affects progressively more of a finite phenomenon through some interval at whose endpoint the process stops and all of the phenomenon is affected. The operational morpheme shifts the time at which the process stops from that endpoint to a nearby earlier point, leaving a lesser portion of the phenomenon still unaffected.

And a free open-class example is *fake* as in *fake gun* (Lakoff, 1982). This operational morpheme is keyed to the semantic component of 'function' in the adjoining morpheme's meaning and shifts it from operable to inoperable along a parameter of operability, while leaving intact semantic components pertaining to sensory qualities like appearance or feel.

5.3   Idiomatic (E3)

A third type of combination constitutes an idiom. In it, two or more morphemes with their own meanings combine, largely in accord with rules of morphology or syntax, but this combination is associated with a novel meaning. That is, its overall meaning does not result additively (compositionally) or operationally from the input meanings, though some elements of these types may persist. Idioms are preestablished constructs in a language—not freely generated by a speaker—and so are part of a language's lexicon in the arena of the inventory. Idioms can occur within a multimorphemic word, across free words, and in a complex construction.

An example of an idiomatic multimorphemic word is *untold*—a morphological combination of three morphemes: *un-* 'negative' (different from the *un-* in *untie*), *tell* 'recount', and the past participle indicating a passive-like focus shift to the Patient. The overall concept associated with this word is 'vast', which cannot be derived from its morphemic components.

An example of an idiom composed of free words is *have it out with*, whose overall meaning, again not derivable from its components, is '[for X to] finally air openly with [Y] an implicit dispute that had been growing between X and Y'. All the components conform with syntactic rules except that the *it*, usually an anaphor, has no target.

And an example of an idiom consisting of a complex construction is the "modal-request construction" seen in *Can you pass me the salt? / Could you all please sign in? / Won't you take a seat, please?*. Somewhat simplified, the general pattern of the construction can be represented as in (10), where at most one instance of *please* can occur. This construction is an idiom because the meanings of its components do not combine into the concept of a request. However, some of the input meanings are consistent with that concept. Thus, the meaning of the interrogative intonation pattern is itself a request, though one for a verbal response, and the futurity of *will* is consistent with the fact that the hearer's response follows the request.

(10)   *can/will* INDICATIVE/CONDITIONAL POSITIVE/NEGATIVE
       you SINGULAR/PLURAL (*please*) VP (*please*) DECLARATIVE/
       INTERROGATIVE-INTONATION

5.4 Constructively Discrepant (E4)

A fourth type of combination again lies in the arena of expression. In it, the speaker intentionally combines linguistic elements that are conceptually incompatible with each other. The hearer can discern that a discrepancy is present. But the speaker intends that this discrepancy will initiate a process of resolution in the hearer that, through certain cognitive operations he performs, will yield the coherent conceptual complex that she had intended to convey. This type of combination can accordingly be characterized as "constructive discrepancy" (T12 c14).

Such constructive discrepancy is the basis for all tropes, as well as some linguistic phenomena not usually classed as tropes. Such tropes and other phenomena can be divided into two types based on whether the conceptual discrepancy is between morphemes within the utterance or between the utterance and general knowledge. These "inner-conflict" and "outer-conflict" types are discussed next in order.

5.4.1 Conflict between Morphemes (E4a)

In the inner-conflict type of constructive discrepancy, the speaker intentionally combines morphemes whose standard meanings conflict with each other and so disaccord with rules of coherence. The hearer reconciles these conflicts, largely through general knowledge, using a certain range of semantic operations (T2 c5). The illustrations that follow are sequenced by the type of operation required.

5.4.1.1 Concept Insertion (E4a1)

One operation a hearer can perform to reconcile discrepant meanings is "concept insertion". The tropes of the type under discussion here indicate their presence to a hearer through semantic conflict between morphemes, and a subset of these relies on this operation for resolution.

One trope of this type is metonymy (e.g., Radden and Kövecses, 2007), which largely rests on specifying an action together with an entity that cannot perform the action—hence the discrepancy—but that is related to the entity that can perform it. The hearer can resolve the discrepancy by conceptually adding in the relation of the latter entity to the former. Thus, in *The ham sandwich just left without paying*, the conflict lies in the hearer's knowledge that a sandwich cannot leave or pay. But he can resolve this conflict in his cognition by inserting the concept 'the person who had ordered' before the concept represented by *the ham sandwich*.

Another trope in the same subset is fictive motion, which predicates motion of a stationary object (T1 c2). An example is *The fence goes from the plateau down into the valley* [4.1.1 (D1a1)]. A hearer can reconcile this by inserting the concept 'one's focus of attention in scanning along' before the concept represented by *the fence*.

What might also be considered a trope in this subset is coercion (Pustejovsky, 1995), where the conflict generally involves a mismatch in grammatical agreement. Though underrecognized, coercion can also occur within a multimorphemic word, like the final one in *Our experiment uses several nitrogens*. The suffix *-s* standardly combines with a count noun having a uniplex referent and multiplexes that referent, but here it is combined with a mass noun. The hearer may resolve this discrepancy through concept insertion, here adding the notion of different types (e.g., isotopes) or multiple units (e.g., molecules), as if the phrase were reworded as *several types/units of nitrogen*.

5.4.1.2   *Concept Adaptation (E4a2)*

An additional reconciling operation is "concept adaptation". It can be seen in metaphor—another trope that identifies itself through semantic conflict between its constituents—where the concepts of a source domain are structurally aligned with and adapted to the concepts of a target domain (e.g., Lakoff, 1993).

An example *is I'm lurching through my term paper*. The conflict is between the verb *lurch*, which refers to a person in physical space stepping jerkily ahead in short irregular bursts punctuated by halts, and the nominal *term paper*, which refers to a written composition on an academic topic. But the hearer may resolve these by adapting the former concepts to the latter where they now consist of short irregular bursts of activity, punctuated by periods of inactivity, and without progression in a concerted thematic direction (T12 s14.4.1).

The operation of concept adaptation has a close variant in "cue adaptation", used where the combination of cues in a speaker's act of targeting are in conflict. Consider, for example, a woman who sits across a restaurant table from a man and, while looking at his mouth, says *You've got something in your teeth right here* and gestures by touching her own teeth (T12 s14.1). The hearer/viewer recognizes the conflict between, on the one hand, the core cue from the deictic *here* and the gestural cue from her pointing finger, both indicating the speaker as the target, and, on the other hand, the co-form cue from the phrase *in your teeth* and the ocular cue from the speaker's line-of-sight, both indicating the hearer as the target. The hearer resolves this conflict by adapting the former set of cues to the latter, as if the woman instead had said *there* and had pointed toward his teeth.

5.4.1.3 Concept Blending (E4a3)

Another operation that a hearer (or viewer) can perform on conflicting concepts associated with different morphemes in a sentence (or parts of an image) is to generate a conceptual blend that joins portions of each into a single conceptual structure (Fauconnier and Turner, 1996). This operation is generally also at work in a metaphor in conjunction with the operation of concept adaptation, since the latter does not act thoroughly without a trace (if it did, a metaphor would be indistinguishable from its literal counterpart). Thus, in the "lurching" metaphor example above, the hearer probably does not convert the physical gait totally into a type of authorial progress but may also construct a blended image. The image here might consist of, say, the speaker corporeally lurching along on a field consisting of a giant physicalized term paper.

5.4.1.4 Concept Cancelation (E4a4)

A further reconciling operation is "concept cancelation" (T4 s4.3). It is seen in an example like *The shopping cart rolled across the boulevard and was hit by an oncoming car*. The preposition *across* in its dynamic sense prototypically refers to a point-like Figure moving horizontally from one edge perpendicularly to the opposite edge of a planar Ground bounded by two parallel edges. But the second clause introduces a conflict: the cart did not reach the other side. The hearer resolves this conflict by canceling the concept 'to the opposite edge', otherwise part of the preposition's meaning.

5.4.1.5 Concept Stretching (E4a5)

Yet another reconciling operation is "concept stretching". To illustrate it, we first note that the meaning of the preposition *across* includes an additional concept not cited in the characterization just above: the length of the Figure's perpendicular path is less than or equal to that of the edges. This concept is complied with in *I swam across the river / square pool from one side to the other*. But it is moderately conflicted with in *I swam across the oblong pool from one end to the other*. The hearer, however, can resolve this conflict by stretching the permitted ratios of the two axes just a bit. It cannot be stretched too much, though, as seen in the unacceptability of **I swam across the river from one end to the other*.

Constructive discrepancy in language affords a number of advantages. Concept insertion permits a shortened utterance. Concept adaptation permits a quick setting up of an analogy. And concept cancelation and stretching permit a much smaller lexicon. Here, for example, English does not need multiply different prepositions for each slight geometric variation.

5.4.2 Conflict between Utterance and General Knowledge (E4b)

In the second type of constructive discrepancy, the speaker intentionally produces an utterance that is internally unconflicted—its literal compositional meaning affords no problem—but that conflicts with general knowledge. This discrepant combination again leads the hearer to undertake a reconciling operation.

Certain tropes rest on this type of discrepancy. Two such tropes are hyperbole and sarcasm, both of which in fact call on the hearer for a still further type of reconciling operation, "concept rescaling".

Hyperbole is illustrated by a speaker saying *I met the most interesting person on the planet last night*. The hearer's knowledge that the speaker does not know all the world's people and that encountering a pinnacle among them is improbable leads him to assess the utterance as a trope of hyperbole and hence to scale the superlative most (... on the planet)' down to just 'very'. That is, along a scale of interestingness which, from a neutral point, rises into a positive zone and descends into a negative zone, the virtually topmost point specified by the utterance is conceptually relocated downward to a much lower point, though one still in the positive zone and well above the neutral point.

Sarcasm is illustrated by a speaker who, on seeing a friend trip in climbing the stairs to her door, says *That was graceful*. Here, the hearer realizes that the conceptual content represented by her utterance conflicts with what he knows the actuality of his actions to have been and concludes that it was a trope of sarcasm. He reconciles the literal content of her utterance with the different conceptual complex she presumably had in mind through another operation of downscaling, here along a scale of gracefulness. But for this trope, unlike that of hyperbole, the shift takes the overtly indicated point in the positive zone down past the neutral point into the negative zone, here, that of clumsiness.

6 Diachronic Comparison (F)

Another major means for investigating how language structures conceptual content is to compare its attributes across its different instantiations. Such instantiations can consist of different stages in the temporal continuum of a single language under a diachronic comparison, as discussed here. Or it can consist of a single stage within different languages under a crosslinguistic comparison, as discussed under the next category [7]. Where the next category will include a comparison of different dialects separated geographically, the present category compares different "chronolects" separated temporally.

Diachronic comparison is one branch of a larger category of "time scope" whose other branch is synchronic analysis. This other branch covers any analysis of a language at a single stage of its existence. Most of the descriptions in this book are in fact cast in synchronic terms.

As for the diachronic branch, comparison can show that some aspects of language—linguistic universals [7.1]—never change. But all other aspects of language can change. There are several major parameters of such change that could have formed the basis for organizing the present discussion, for example, the different causes of change such as analogy and borrowing. But the parameter selected here has received less attention—the time scale over which different types of change tend to occur, from long to short, discussed next in order. The investigation of what in language can change and what cannot and, in the case of change, the time scale over which it takes place can reveal much about cognitive organization.

6.1 Long Time Scale (F1)

One seemingly long-term aspect of language is its "body plan"—the patterns in which it characteristically arranges conceptual content [4.2] in certain classes of propositions.

In one of the most enduring classes present in Indo-European languages from the earliest records of them to the present day, this language family seems to have maintained the same basic pattern for representing a proposition of "object maneuvering" (T2 c4 s2). In this pattern, a subject and direct-object noun phrase respectively represent the Agent and the Figure—the maneuvered object—while the verb represents the maneuvering.

This pattern is seen in *I threw/kicked/carried/brought/took/pushed/pulled/held/had the ball* as well as in *I gave her the ball* and *I put the ball in the box*. The verb can represent such different aspects of maneuvering as phase and direction of placement: *hold / put / take (the ball in/into/out of the box)*; transport: *carry / bring / take (the ball to a neighbor)*; instrument: *throw / kick / bat*; force: *push / pull*; deixis: *bring / take (the ball to a neighbor)*; and possession: *have / give / take (the ball to/from a friend)*.

Though this pattern may be continuous in Indo-European languages and seem inevitable to their speakers, Atsugewi presents quite a different body plan, possibly one of some time depth since forms of it appear in other Hokan languages. To begin with, Atsugewi simply lacks all verb roots with meanings like those of *have, give, take, hold, put, carry, bring, throw, kick, push,* and *pull*.

Instead, the verb root characteristically represents a particular type of Figure object or material as moving or located, for example, *-qput* 'for dirt to move/be located'. Different "instrumental" prefixes represent concepts like those of throwing, kicking, pushing, and pulling as prior events causal of the Figure's motion or location. Different directional suffixes represent concepts of placement and transport as paths or locations of the Figure relative to a Ground entity—e.g., *-ićt* '(a figure moving) into liquid'. This set of suffixes also includes three that represent the concepts of 'having', 'giving', and 'taking (from)' as directional concepts. These can be respectively glossed as 'in (the subject's) possession', 'into (the direct object's) possession', and 'out of (the direct object's) possession'. And two deictic suffixes represent the direction of motion as toward or not toward the speaker.

The Atsugewi pattern is so thoroughgoing that verb roots also represent body parts and garments as moving or located Figures. These verb roots occur within multi-affixal verbs equivalent to such English object-maneuvering sentences as *I stuck my ear against the wall* and *I took my shoes off*.

Somewhat less abiding, though still on a longer time scale, is the class of propositions that represent a macro-event [5.1.4] and that are subject to the framing typology [7.3] (T2 c3, T10). A proposition of this class places a "coevent" in a particular relation with a "framing event". The framing event can express Motion, temporal contouring, state change, action correlating, or realization. The typology is based on where the "core schema" of the framing event—for example, the Path of a Motion event—is represented. It is characteristically represented in the verb in a "verb-framed" language and in the satellite and/or adposition and/or noun affix in a "satellite-framed" language. But a language can undergo a typological shift. Thus, while Indo-European has been satellite-framed from the earliest languages through to many present-day ones, the lineage descended from Latin shifted to being verb-framed in all the Romance languages. And the reverse typological shift has taken place in the continuum from Archaic Chinese to modern Mandarin (Li, 2018).

Comparably, some areal phenomena—linguistic patterns common across neighboring but unrelated languages and hence borrowed by some languages from others—seem to be realized over a longer time scale. For example, a wide swath of languages from different families, perhaps centered in northern California, have a set of "instrumental prefixes" that mainly represent the immediate cause of the event expressed by the verb root. Mithun (2007) proposes that what was borrowed was a pattern in which an open-class verb root is first preceded by other open-class roots that—over some time—codify into a closed set of prefixes.

One issue needing attention in such longer time scale shifts—as well as in medium scale ones—is whether the change takes place gradually over the interval or comparatively quickly at the end of the interval.

6.2 *Medium Time Scale (F2)*

Certain types of semantic change seem to take place over a medium time scale. One type seems to be the loss of a sense from a morpheme's polysemous range (unlike the apparent swiftness of a sense gain [6.3]). A possible example is seen in the verb *mind*, whose strongest sense is 'object (to)', as in *Do you mind the smoke / if I smoke?*. But another sense, 'be careful about', seems to be on the wane in the U.S. (though apparently still strong in the U.K.), so that *Mind the branches* would be likelier expressed as *Watch out for the branches*. Still, this sense remains available to U.S. hearers, who would probably settle on it in the relevant context.

Another possible medium-scale type is a change in the particular preposition associated with an open-class word, often accompanied by a shift in conceptualization. Though needing confirmation, possible examples include a seeming shift from an older *immune to* to a newer *immune from*; from *ask [a question] of [a person]* to *ask [a question] to [a person]*; from *glad of* to *glad about*; and from (U.S.) *different from* to *different than*.

Another possible medium-scale type is grammaticalization (e.g., Bybee, 2014), in which a morpheme shifts in its categorization from open class to closed class and, through "semantic bleaching", loses some of its originally associated conceptual content. Whatever the semantic starting point, the final meaning must lie within the universally available repertory of closed-class concepts [7.3].

An example is modern English *may*, which derives from an Old English fully inflected verb meaning 'have the power to' but is now a modal that, in its epistemic sense, expresses the possibility, outside the speaker's knowledge, of either the actuality or the nonactuality of a proposition, as seen in *I'll check—there may be some jam left*.

Language change can also arise through borrowing from an influencing language, and some such changes occur on a short time scale, for example the adoption of a foreign word with its original meaning. But other changes seem to occur over a medium scale, as seen with regard to verb satellite meanings in Yiddish among Slavic languages (T2 c4). One such medium scale change is the borrowing of (most of) a polysemous range. Thus, the polysemous range of the Yiddish verb satellite *on-* came to resemble that of Slavic *na-* by losing some originally Germanic senses, gaining several Slavic senses, and retaining the senses already in common. Another such change is the adoption of a concept represented by a whole lexical category. Thus, while Yiddish verb satellites shared with their Slavic counterparts the representation of Path, Yiddish borrowed their systematic use as well for the indication of perfective aspect. And one more such change is the adoption of obligatoriness in the representation of a certain concept when it is present. Thus, Yiddish borrowed from its Slavic neighbors the requirement to mark perfectivity when present, largely through the use of its satellites.

6.3 Short Time Scale (F3)

The type of semantic change occurring over the shortest time scale may consist of certain kinds of addition to a language's lexicon, mostly with respect to open-class forms.

One kind is the addition of a sense to the polysemous range of a morphemic shape. For example, the morphemic shape *bug*, after its 'insect' sense, added the sense 'defect' and later the sense 'concealed microphone'.

A second kind of addition to a language's lexicon is the new use of a morphemic shape in a lexical category other than its usual one. For example, beyond its traditional use as a verb, the form *ask* has recently been used as a noun meaning '(a) request' (*My ask to you is to tell someone about this show*).

And a third kind of lexical addition is a novel morphemic shape with a new sense. An example is *pizzazz* 'appealing dynamic flair in a personality'.

7 Crosslinguistic Comparison (G)

The present category continues the last category's comparison of conceptual structures across different instantiations of language. But here the instantiations consist of a single stage within different languages or varieties of a language under a crosslinguistic comparison, rather than of different stages within a single language under a diachronic comparison.

Crosslinguistic comparison is one branch of a larger category of "language span" whose other branch is single-language analysis, that is, an analysis of any single language or variety of a language. Many of the descriptions in this book are in fact cast in single-language terms.

7.1 Scope of Comparison (G1)

Crosslinguistic comparison can be conducted over a range of scopes from smaller to larger. It might even be extended, at the smallest scope, to within a single individual. Thus, seemingly every individual is at least a "multi-code" speaker, able to use different contextually based variants of her language in accord with the situation—her capacity for "code switching" (Gumperz, 1976). An individual, further, can be multilingual, and a "crosslinguistic" comparison here can perform a cognitive analysis of her differing capabilities with each of her languages.

Several successive increases in scope involve comparisons across related varieties or languages. Thus, at the next larger scope, a comparison can be made across individuals who speak the same sociolect but do so with distinct idiolects—a study of individual differences. At a still larger scope is a comparison across groups of individuals that speak different sociolects of the same dialect within a single community—a study within sociolinguistics (e.g., Geeraerts, 2016). Larger yet is a comparison across different geographically separated dialects of the same language—a study within dialectology. Finally, comparisons can be made of related languages in the same language family, often involving diachrony since the differences largely result from changes in a common proto-language.

At a much larger scope are comparisons across the languages of the world regardless of their family membership. Such comparisons can uncover aspects of language that differ in their degree of commonality from total to lacking. Four such degrees are discussed next in order: absolutely universal, typological, repertorial, and indefinitely diverse (T7). All suggestions here about degree of commonality are heuristic pending extensive crosslinguistic investigation.

7.2 Absolutely Universal (G2)

Absolute universals are linguistic phenomena manifested in all languages. We next address positive universals, negative universals, and explanations for universality.

7.2.1 Positive Universals (G2a)

An absolute linguistic universal is positive if it holds that something is present in all languages. Many of the linguistic phenomena already discussed in this taxonomy are in fact themselves absolute positive universals. A number of these are identified next because of their significance to linguistic theory.

Thus, all languages have the three divisions of form, grammar, and meaning. All have morphemes—minimal meaning-associated constructs—that mostly associate all three divisions. All have both open-class and closed-class categories of morphemes. All have morpheme types consisting of segment combinations, intonation contours, idiomatic combinations, constituent categories, grammatical relations, phrase structures, and constructions. All have morphemes with a polysemous/homophonous set of senses. And all have both a lexicon and expression as arenas of morpheme assembly.

All languages have speech participation by speaker and hearer. All have a system of turn taking that alternates the speaker's and hearer's processes of production and interpretation. All have speaker selection of what to express explicitly and how to express it so as to represent a larger conceptual complex.

All have hearer inference of the implicit remainder of such a complex as well as hearer resolution of polysemy. All have a distinction between explicit semantics and inferential pragmatics. And all use context of the same range of types in the preceding processes.

All languages use the meanings of closed-class morphemes to structure conceptual content in a particular range of schematic systems. These systems—themselves possibly absolute universals that always include or exclude certain concepts or conceptual categories—include the configurational structure of space and time, perspective point, the distribution of attention, force dynamics (including causation), cognitive state, reality status, communicative purpose, ontology, role semantics, and quantity. And all languages pattern conceptual content in their morphemes, lexicons, and expressions. The morphemes' overall meanings are partitioned into a core meaning consisting of semantic components and an associated meaning that can include a holistic, infrastructure, collateral, disposition, or attitude sector. The lexicons have particular morpheme class sizes and inter-morphemic relations. And the expressions have particular patterns in which content is arranged.

All languages combine semantic units in accord with four different patterns, ones that are additive, operational, idiomatic, and constructively discrepant. In all languages, further, their additive pattern includes a hierarchy that, from lower to higher, consists of the meanings of semantic components, morphemes, phrases, clauses, sentences, one-speaker discourses, and interchanges. And their pattern of constructive discrepancy includes all tropes, both ones based on a semantic conflict between morphemes and ones based on a semantic conflict between literal meaning and general knowledge.

Finally, all languages change, and can do so with respect to any linguistic features except their universals, with some features changing more slowly and some more quickly. And across all languages, children tend to follow the same general temporal outline in the acquisition of their native language [8.1.2].

7.2.2 Negative Universals (G2b)

An absolute linguistic universal is negative if it holds that something is absent from all languages. Though negative universals are excluded from the design of language, significantly, they can help bring that design into relief. We here present a representative sample out of a perhaps indefinitely large number.

Thus, 1) no language requires that an interchange, in addition to a speaker and hearer, must include a monitor directing their exchange of utterances. 2) A language's lexicon, even with polysemous senses counted, has entries numbering in the multiple thousands but not millions. 3) In no language can agreement between two constituents—say, between an adjective and a noun—be indicated by a speaker's on-the-spot choice of a particular affix placed on both constituents. 4) Seemingly no language has a closed-class form used to mark a constituent as an antecedent about to be referred back to by an anaphor (*Bob and Tom-um were standing together—I walked up to him).

Further, 5) speaking the words of a sentence in reverse order to represent a concept, say, the negation of its proposition, is not a possible type of morpheme. 6) Verb roots in a language can be lexicalized to express aspect but apparently never tense. Thus, English cannot have a verb *to went* meaning 'to go in the past' so that *I am wenting* would mean 'I was going'. 7) Monomorphemic triggers (deictics or anaphors)—e.g., *there* 'at that location' *then* 'at that time'—can target phenomena over a wide ontological range [4.1.8]. But they seemingly never target many other types of phenomena such as those in 'at that distance' or 'with that frequency' (T12 s3.2). And 8) no co-speech gesture system requires a fixed indicator, say, the left thumb, pointing at the intended gesture, say, the right hand extending forward, to inform the viewer which body part to focus on (T12 s5.1.2).

A number of additional negative universals are proposed in the sections that follow.

7.2.3 Explanations of Universality (G2c)

Each degree of crosslinguistic commonality calls for cognitive explanation. Though this is scarcely available at present, several bases can be proposed to account for those aspects of language that are universal. One basis might be that 1) in the lineage leading to humans, there evolved a cognitive system specifically organized for language that provides its universal properties. Another possible basis is that 2) processes operating generally throughout cognition and the various systems in it also operate in our language capacity and alone determine universal properties there without need for specifically linguistic processes. A further basis is that 3) those properties that are common across all languages fulfill functions that simply cannot be fulfilled any other way and so occur by necessity. Yet another possible basis is that 4) the earliest language to appear happened to have certain characteristics, a number of which have simply remained in all its daughter languages.

Perhaps the complements of these bases can account for the nonuniversal aspects of language. That is, languages can and readily do diverge wherever no constraints arise 1) from an evolved language system; 2) from general cognitive processes; 3) from the exigencies of internal or external circumstances; or 4) from an original ur-language.

7.3   Typological (G3)

A "typology" consists of a linguistic category with relatively few members. The category itself has absolutely universal representation—at least one of its members must appear in every language—but none of its members is universal.[8] Rather, each member appears in only some subset of languages. Where it appears in a language, it is typically the only or the main member of the category there, and it is "characteristic" there, that is, it is colloquial, frequent, and pervasive (present across a range of subtypes) (T2 c1). While the members of a typology are not universal, they are "universally available"—each member *could* be adopted by a language and is adopted by some languages.

We can illustrate with two related semantic typologies, both involving Motion. The "framing typology" (already discussed in [4.2.2], [5.1.4], and [6.1]) is based on where the Path component from the semantic tier characteristically appears on the syntactic tier. This category of syntactic location has two main members. Path is characteristically represented either in a language's verb root ("verb-framed") or in a satellite and/or adposition and/or noun affix ("satellite-framed").

Complementarily, the "actuating typology" (T2 c1, T11) is based on which component from the semantic tier characteristically appears in the verb root on the syntactic tier. This category of semantic alternatives has three main members. Most languages characteristically place the Path, the coevent, or the Figure in the verb root—as seen respectively in Spanish, English, and Atsugewi.

The members of a typological category can exhibit a crosslinguistic prevalence hierarchy [8.2.1]. Thus, within the actuating typology, a Path verb system seems to be the commonest across languages, a coevent verb system somewhat less common, and a Figure verb system rather uncommon.

Further, a typology can be conceptually extended to allow consideration of potential alternatives that in fact do not occur. Such alternatives then fall at the zero level of the prevalence hierarchy and can be added to the inventory of negative universals [7.1.2]. In the actuating typology, for example, no language characteristically uses its verb to express the Ground, nor a combination of two different Motion components, nor the concept of Motion alone without an additional component from the semantic tier.

---

8   A universal category can have members that are also universal, but then it is not a typology. An example is the category of combination, with its four members: additive, operational, idiomatic, and constructively discrepant [5]. All four members are present in every language.

7.4 Repertorial (G4)

A "repertory" consists of a linguistic category with relatively numerous members. The category itself tends to have universal representation and its members tend not to, but the opposites of these tendencies can also occur. As in a typology, the members of a repertory are universally available.

A typology and a repertory differ in certain respects. First, each language generally selects just one member of a small typological category for its characteristic use, and many languages are alike in selecting the same one. But, in accord with some principle of representativeness, each language selects its own distinct subset of the many members in a repertory.

Second, much like a typology, a repertory can exhibit a prevalence hierarchy among its members—down to members that are plausible but that never occur in any language. However, unlike a typology, it can also include members that occur in every language and that can accordingly be added to the set of absolute positive universals [7.1.1].

Finally, while the membership of a typology is wholly closed, that of a repertory is only preponderantly closed. A prevalence hierarchy can extend ever lower to rare members occurring in perhaps only one language.

One possible example of a repertory is the category of all tropes, which—depending on the analysis—can number in the scores if not the hundreds (Baldrick, 2008). A coarse-grained glance that disregards any categories among them suggests that different subsets of these tropes, but never all of them, are found across different languages as spoken colloquially at any given time. Seemingly some tropes—perhaps metaphor and metonymy—occur universally. Others may be rare. One example might be that of "pretend addressee", as where, say, a mother standing alone with her son looks off to one side as if addressing someone there and says *Is he going to take out the garbage? Nooo*.

Other repertories involve the mechanism of closed-class semantics [4.1]. As seen, this mechanism has three levels. From the more general to the more specific, certain schematic systems each contain certain conceptual categories, each of which in turn contains certain basic semantic components. The meanings of all the closed-class morphemes in the world's languages consist of particular selections from among these semantic components, arranged in particular structured patterns. The whole mechanism as well as each of these three levels is a repertory. Each level is next discussed in turn.

7.4.1 The Level of Schematic Systems (G4a)

At the highest level, all ten of the schematic systems discussed in [4.1] may prove to be absolutely universal, represented by closed-class forms in all languages. But other candidates for schematic system status would not be.

Thus, a potential schematic system of "status" might be common but it is not universal—English for one language lacks closed-class representation of it. And if "rate" can be regarded as a schematic system, it is a rare one, represented in only a few languages by verb affixes for 'fast' and 'slow'.

Further, indefinitely many candidates for schematic system status may be excluded as absolute negative universals. Some candidates are excluded even though they have a structural function in cognitive systems outside language. An example might be a seemingly absent schematic system of "sensory qualia" in that, crosslinguistically, there is apparently no closed-class marking of visual categories like color or brightness, auditory categories like loudness or pitch, or haptic categories like soft/hard or smooth/rough. And certainly no schematic systems exist for such conceptual categories as types of work or of food—open-class forms may but closed-class forms do not mark distinctions there.

7.4.2 The Level of Conceptual Categories within a Schematic System (G4b)

At the next level down, within a schematic system, some conceptual categories may well be absolute universals. An example within the schematic system of communicative purpose may be the conceptual category of questioning if in fact every language has some closed-class interrogative marking.

But it seems possible—given that English has so little closed-class representation of it—that, within the schematic system of cognitive state, the conceptual category of affect may be common but not universal.

And at the negative end, the schematic system of configurational structure seems to lack a conceptual category of absolute magnitude—at least within the spatial domain—even though it does have a category of relative magnitude. For example, while some languages like English have different deictics that distinguish proximal from distal with respect to relative distance from the speaker, apparently none have deictics that distinguish absolute distances of, say, inches vs. parsecs. This nondiscrimination is seen in *This speck is smaller than that speck* and *This planet is smaller than that planet*, where the same closed-class morphemes *this* and *that* serve for objects regardless of their absolute distance away.

7.4.3 The Level of Semantic Components within a Conceptual Category (G4c)

Finally, within conceptual categories, some semantic components may be absolutely universal. For example, in the schematic system of reality status,

A TAXONOMY OF COGNITIVE SEMANTICS   67

under the conceptual category "known as unrealized", the semantic component 'negative' may well have closed-class representation in every language. But in the schematic system of quantity, under the conceptual category of number, the semantic component 'trial' is not universal but in fact rare. And at the negative end, the number concepts 'odd', 'even', 'dozen', and 'countable' are seemingly never represented by closed-class elements.

It can be difficult to distinguish between concepts wholly excluded from closed-class representation and ones able to occur sporadically in the trailing off portion of a repertory. Still, English does provide an example of the latter in the conceptual category of configurational structure, specifically in the spatial domain. The use of *in* vs. *on* for location within a vehicle—as in *in a car / on a bus, in a helicopter / on a plane, in a boat / on a ship, in a caboose / on a train*—distinguishes whether the vehicle respectively lacks or has a walkway. This is an unusual concept to be represented by a closed-class form, perhaps unique to English.

7.5   Indefinitely Diverse (G5)

At the lowest degree of commonality, the contents of some linguistic categories are indefinitely diverse crosslinguistically. Every language has a unique realization of such categories. Seemingly most if not all of such categories involve the semantics of open-class forms—that is, apart from those aspects with a role in the content-structuring mechanism [4.2]. The diversity is present in the meanings of morphemes, their ranges of applicability, their polysemies, and their partitioning of semantic areas, discussed next in order.

7.5.1   Morphemic Meaning (G5a)

A comparison of different languages' lexicons can address the category consisting of the meanings of their open-class morphemes. Crosslinguistically, these meanings do not belong to an absolutely universal, a typological, or even a repertorial set but rather can differ enormously.

To illustrate with one pair of languages, a complete semantic correspondence between an Atsugewi and an English morpheme is relatively uncommon. For example, the Atsugewi verb root *-p̓-* might be glossed as: 'for a planar fabric to move in a way that changes its pattern of bunching'. When combined with different instrumental and directional affixes, this verb root can refer to straightening a dress bunched up under one while sitting, opening curtains, or putting on socks.

Or again, the Atsugewi verb root *-swal-*, which can be glossed as 'for a linear flexible object suspended at one end to move/be located', can occur with different affixes to refer to walking along while carrying dead rabbits strung down from one's belt, sliding a snake away by suspending it under the head with the end of a stick, pants blowing down from a clothesline, or having one's penis hang limp. These verb roots and many others clearly have little semantic correspondence to English morphemes of any lexical category.

It might be thought that certain substantive concepts would be represented by open-class morphemes across all languages on the grounds that human cognition or our encounter with the world is structured in a way that inevitably forms unitizing boundaries around particular portions of the phenomenal continuum. Still, many candidate concepts do not prove out. Thus, an action seemingly as basic as ingesting food, though represented by a single morpheme in both English *eat* and Atsugewi *am-*, has no single morpheme to represent it in Navajo, which instead divides the action into a number of types represented by distinct verb roots depending on characteristics of the food and how it is eaten (Young and Morgan, 1992).

7.5.2 Range of Applicability (G5b)
Even where particular morphemes across two languages share certain aspects of their references, those references can differ in their "range of applicability". For example, the English words *friend* and *acquaintance* share much of their senses with Yiddish *fraynt* and *bakanter*. But if strength of comradeship can be conceptualized as diminishing radially outward from a center point, then the circle enclosing the meaning of English *friend* is wider than that for Yiddish *fraynt*—it has a greater range of applicability.

Range of applicability can also change from one stage of a language to another. Thus, several decades ago U.S. English *girl* could be used to refer to a female person from infancy to early middle age, but now only to the later teens.

7.5.3 Polysemous Range (G5c)
Another class of linguistic phenomena is the set of polysemous/homonymous senses associated with a single morphemic shape. A crosslinguistic comparison suggests that even if all the senses of a particular morphemic shape in one language are expressed as the same senses in another language, they will likely fall in the polysemous ranges of different morphemic shapes there. Thus, consider the English noun *stock* whose polysemous range includes the senses 'financial instrument', 'soup base', 'certain rifle part', 'stored supplies', 'line of descendants', 'farm animals', and 'certain plant species'. It seems unlikely that all these senses would be expressed by the same morphemic shape in another language.

Both polysemy and range of applicability are combined in another example, which demonstrates their sheer idiosyncrasy and unlikely recurrence. In the polysemous range of the English verb *arrest*, one sense can be glossed as 'legally detain to prevent freedom of movement', but it has application only to sufficiently adult live humans: *The police arrested the man/ *goat / *baby / *corpse / *getaway car.* Another sense is 'stop the body-intrinsic growth of', but it applies only to unhealthy tissue: *The medical treatment arrested his tumor / *hair / *nails.* And a third sense is 'hold fixed through allure and thus prevent wandering', but it applies only to a cognitive faculty prone to instantly shifting its state: *The unusual painting arrested my attention/*interest/*observation.*

7.5.4   Partitioning of a Semantic Area (G5d)
A consequence of crosslinguistic discorrespondence in the three preceding aspects of morphemic meaning is that any given semantic area is likely to be divided up in different patterns. Consider the semantic area of one person encountering and engaging another. For part of its system, English uses the verb *meet* either for 1) making someone's acquaintance for the first time (*I met the new principal*) or for 2) conducting a prearranged appointment (*I met my lawyer in her office*). It uses the expression *run into* for 3) a chance encounter (*I ran into an old friend downtown*). And it uses *see* either for 4) a get-together with someone already known (*I saw my uncle today—we had lunch together*) or for 5) certain client-professional encounters (*I saw my doctor today*).

Yiddish partitions this semantic area differently. For part of its system, it uses *bakenen zikh mit* for the first type of encounter, *trefn zikh mit* for the second and fourth type, *bagegenen* for the third, and *geyn tsu* or *zayn mit* for the fifth.

Differences between languages in their typological and repertorial selections as well as in their inventories of morpheme meanings and polysemous groupings make exact translation a near impossibility.

8   Quantity of Manifestation (H)

Linguistically represented conceptual content can have a greater or lesser quantity of manifestation either in elaboratedness or in prevalence, discussed next in order. In general, the greater the quantity, the more that cognition and its processes are engaged. Certain manifestations of quantity, further, can change through time.

8.1   *Elaboratedness (H1)*
Linguistically represented conceptual content can be more or less elaborated, that is, more or less comprehensive and granular. This category can be seen at work in four venues—in a communication system, in a language user, in a

lexicon, and in expression—discussed next in order. This parameter can pertain to the entirety of an expressive capacity (as in the first two subsections below) or to a particular conceptual category or idea (as in the second two subsections).

8.1.1   In a Communication System (H1a)

The conceptual content that a communication system as a whole can represent can be more or less elaborated. Specifically, it can be more or less comprehensive in the total amount of ideation that it can represent and granular in the fineness and number of the conceptual distinctions that it can make.

Different communication systems have varying degrees of conceptual elaboration. In very roughly increasing order, these include a plant or nonhuman animal communication system; a smaller devised limited system such as emoji; body language, facial expression, and gesture; a larger devised limited system such as Basic English; home sign; a pidgin; a heritage language; and "restricted code" (Bernstein, 1964). Toward the top of the scale, a great degree of conceptual elaboration is seen in every spoken or signed language with a sufficiently long history.

A communication system's degree of conceptual elaboratedness can increase, as when a pidgin develops into a creole, or when the signed language originally developed by the initial group of deaf students in Nicaragua turned into the full system of the later students (Kegl et al., 1999). And it can decrease, as in "language death"—that is, where a speech community's competence with an inherited language declines as that language is gradually replaced.

8.1.2   In a Language User (H1b)

Individuals can also exhibit different degrees of conceptual elaboratedness in their language. A lesser degree is seen in a language learner at any stage in acquiring an L1 or L2. It is also present due to deficit, whether developmental, as through reduced exposure or deprivation during childhood, or biological, as with congenital language disorders. By contrast, great elaboration is seen in any fully fluent speaker.

Individual conceptual elaboration increases during language acquisition, as when the language of an L1 learner moves toward an adult level (e.g., Tomasello, 2010) or that of an L2 learner moves toward a native level (e.g., Robinson and Ellis, 2008). Such increase might also be invoked where the written language of an author evolves over her career. And it can decrease, as when a speaker becomes rusty in a language once known well, or in the case of a later-onset language disorder.

8.1.3 In a Lexicon (H1c)

In the lexicon of a language, a particular conceptual category can range from being greatly elaborated, with many members making fine distinctions, down to being minimally represented. This issue was already discussed in [4.2.2] for the much greater elaboration of Manner verbs and Path prepositions in English than in Spanish.

In turn, the fifty-some directional suffixes in the Atsugewi verb mark substantially finer spatial distinctions than English path satellites and prepositions do. For example, Atsugewi has no path suffix with the broad semantic scope of English *in* but rather has the twelve narrower-scoped suffixes in (11).

(11) waw 'into a gravitic container'
     (e.g., a basket)
    -ipsnᵘ 'into a volumetric enclosure' (e.g., a room)
    -wam· 'into an aerial enclosure' (e.g., a corral)
    -isp -u· 'into an aggregate' (e.g., bushes / a crowd)
    -ićt 'into liquid'

    -mić 'into the ground'

    -cisᵘ 'into a raised horizontal surface' (e.g., the top of a tree stump)
    -ik̓s 'into a vertical surface' (e.g., a tree trunk)
    -ik̓sᵘ 'into a corner'

    -tip -u· 'into a large hole in the ground' (e.g., a pit / cellar)
    -ikn 'over a rim into a hole' (e.g., a gopher hole / mouth)
    -mik· 'into someone's face / eye'

For a different domain, consider a lexicon's elaboration of the class of "ideophones" (or "expressives" / "mimetics"). These are morphemes in a sentence that in effect place a hearer vividly in the midst of a referent scene as if able to directly perceive a specific effect there. Japanese has great elaboration of this class (Toratani, 2024), whereas English represents it minimally with just a few instances like *lickety-split* (*The squirrel climbed lickety-split up the tree trunk*) and *kerplunk* (*A coconut from high in the tree landed kerplunk at his feet*).

Pending diachronic confirmation, it may be the case that great elaboration of a particular category in a language arises incrementally from a stage at which the category, perhaps fortuitously, marked a few more distinctions than usual and was then recruited by speakers for expansion.

8.1.4 In Expression (H1d)

A speaker can represent roughly the same conceptual complex with greater or lesser elaboration, that is, she can render it more specific and precise or more general and approximate. The choice of degree can be keyed to the hearer's knowledge about the topic. For example, a speaker addressing a nongardener might say *I used my trowel to dig a hole in the ground, placed the bulb root-end down at the bottom, and filled the hole back up with soil*. But to a fellow gardener, she might instead say *I planted the bulb*.

8.2 Prevalence (H2)

Various kinds of linguistically represented conceptual content can be more or less prevalent, that is, more or less frequent in occurrence. Differences in prevalence can occur across languages or within a single language, as discussed next in order.

8.2.1 Compared across Languages (H2a)

A difference in prevalence across languages was already discussed for the members of a typology or repertory [7.2, 7.3]. What can be added here is that some prevalence differences seem due to particular aspects of cognition—one's involving bias, efficiency, and load, addressed next in order.

8.2.1.1 Cognitive Bias (H2a1)

Cognitive bias can be illustrated with a language's characteristic closed-class marking of number in count nominals. A language can grammatically treat such number as consisting of one, two, three, or four groups. A one-group language basically lacks number marking. A two-group division is seemingly always between the singular on the one hand and the "2-plural" on the other ("n-plural" is here used to refer to n or more units). It is never, say, between two units and a 3-plural. The three-group division is between singular, dual, and a 3-plural, while a four-group division is between singular, dual, trial and a 4-plural.[9]

While it is not yet clear whether languages without number marking or ones with a two-group division are more prevalent, languages with successively more divisions are successively less prevalent. This pattern accords with its further status as an "implicational universal" (Greenberg, 1963)—here holding, for example, that a language with trial marking must also have dual marking. This crosslinguistic prevalence pattern may reflect a particular cognitive bias. This bias would involve locating any divisions within a scale near its low end and making fewer such divisions.

---

9   It is not clear how some languages' "paucal" marking for several units fits this pattern.

8.2.1.2 *Efficiency / Load Bias (H2a2)*
Another prevalence ranking across languages is seen in the actuating typology [7.2] where, in addition to the concept 'MOVE', the verb characteristically seems to express the Path most often, the coevent next most often, the Figure rarely, and the Ground never. No cognitive basis for this ranking is yet obvious. But two excluded patterns may each have such a cognitive basis.

Apparently no language characteristically uses the verb to express just 'MOVE' alone without an additional semantic component of the Motion situation. To do so would be a semantic waste of an obligatory constituent. It may reflect a cognitive tendency against inefficiency. And seemingly no language characteristically uses the verb to express a combination of two components, say, Path and Manner, in addition to 'MOVE'. To do so would require a prohibitive number of distinct lexical items—one for each combination. For example, a lexicon might need to have separate morphemes for moving in/out/up/down/across/around while walking/running/crawling/swimming/flying. The lack of such a pattern might reflect a tendency against an excessive cognitive load on memory.

8.2.2 In a Single Language (H2b)
Prevalence within a single language mainly pertains to the frequency with which various linguistic formations occur in expression ("token frequency") or in the lexicon ("type frequency"), addressed next in order.

8.2.2.1 *In Expression (H2b1)*
In the arena of expression, the assessment of frequency is made not in the production of a single expression but across expressions produced in the aggregate. Prevalence of this kind is directly addressed by the usage-based approach (Langacker, 1988) and is most readily studied through corpus research.

Where certain linguistic formations have comparable semantic effect, the relative frequency with which a speaker selects among them rests in part on a certain property that the formations have in the lexicon: their different degrees of "privilege of occurrence" for a given syntactic or stylistic context. Thus in an informal context, a speaker choosing among lexical alternatives will say *start* more often than *commence* and will perhaps rank the likelihood of referring to great speed with a single morpheme in the following sequence: *fast* > *quick* > *rapid* > *swift* > *fleet*. And a speaker choosing among constructional alternatives will increase the ratio of main clauses to subordinate clauses. A language acquirer learns the privilege of occurrence of such formations by noticing the different frequencies with which speakers use them in different contexts.

8.2.2.2   In the Lexicon (H2b2)

In the arena of the lexicon, prevalence can be seen for example where semantically comparable closed-class forms associate in different proportions with open-class forms. Thus, of the English alternatives for representing the plural of a uniplex count noun, the suffix *-s* (*cats*) is far more prevalent than, say, the suffix *-en* (*oxen*), vowel alteration (*mice*), or zero change (*sheep*).

Such prevalence ratios among a set of closed-class forms is based on their combination with open-class forms already in the lexicon. But the most prevalent closed-class form is generally also the most "productive" one in combinations with new open-class forms. Thus, the plural of *nerd* is *nerds*, not *nerden*.

In addition, the prevalence ratios among the senses of a morpheme can determine whether one sense is a metaphoric extension of another or is simply a further sense within the morpheme's polysemous range. Thus, the use of *foot* to mean 'bottom', as in *foot of the lamp / mountain*, is rare and thus seems metaphoric, but if it were to spread, 'bottom' would come to seem a literal sense within *foot*'s polysemous range.

Diachronic increases and decreases of prevalence in a language's lexicon are pervasive. But in addition, an increase and a decrease can occur in coordination. Thus, consider the spread in English of the termination *-in-law*, which was suffixed to morphemes expressing a consanguineal kinship relation and represented a conceptual operation [5.2] of shift from such a relation to a corresponding affinal kinship relation. This spread correlated with the gradual loss from the lexicon of Old English monomorphemic words that directly represented the affinal relations, such as *sweor* 'father-in-law', *sweger* 'mother-in-law', and *snoru* 'daughter-in-law' (T14 s2.1). This example of frequency change has additional cognitive-semantic significance because it constitutes a switch from a direct to an operational [5.2] type of conceptual representation.

9   Communication Systems (I)

Communication is a process in which one entity, the "sender", executes certain actions that have the function of inducing particular responses in a certain other entity, the "receiver". The sender and the receiver are at different locations. The sender's actions produce certain effects, the "signal", that transit from the sender to the receiver via a particular "medium", and that the receiver can detect (T13 s1.1).

In the basic case, such communication has evolved biologically and can occur between components in a single cell, between single-celled organisms, between cells in a multicellular organism, or between multicellular organisms. And in a derivative case, biological entities already having communication can devise communication systems novel in certain respects (e.g., writing, Morse code, and radio).

While this characterization of communication is general, cognitive semantics is mainly concerned with certain particularizations of it. The sender and receiver are sentient multicellular organisms, preponderantly human. The sender's actions are undertaken volitionally. And the response by the receiver that the sender intends is to experience certain conceptual content in consciousness.[10]

The particular actions that a sender uses to produce a signal and the corresponding sensory modality that the receiver uses to perceive it—where the medium between the two participants can support the signal's transit—define the "channel" or "modality" of a communication.

Thus, spoken language can be said to use the "vocal-auditory" channel, since the sender's actions are vocalizations and the receiver perceives them through hearing. The medium of air here supports the passage of sound. Both co-speech gesture and signed language then use the "somatic-visual" channel, since the sender's actions are visible movements of particular body parts in certain configurations (other than for vocalization), and the receiver perceives them through sight. The medium of air here supports the passage of light. The same channel is used by lip reading, which differs in that the actions of the sender that the receiver focuses on are limited to those of the mouth. The communication system of the deaf-blind in turn uses the "somatic-haptic" channel, especially of a manual-manual kind, where the sender's actions consist of bodily movements and pressures that the receiver perceives through the haptic senses and where the medium of direct contact supports the transmission of such signals. And to simplify its full trajectory, writing uses a visual-visual channel whose medium includes surfaces that support its display and viewing by readers.

In further forms of communication that traditionally are more the purview of semiotics, what is conveyed and appears in the receiver's consciousness is less precise and ideational and more vague and affective or mood-related. Such forms include music, dance, apparel, art, and architecture.

As a complement to the focus of this taxonomy on spoken language in the vocal-auditory channel, the next two subsections respectively address gesture

---

10   The sender's intent need not be for the receiver to simply replicate her own conceptual content. For example, she may structure her signal to induce effects in the hearer such as surprise or suspense [4.2.3] that she herself does not experience.

and signed language in the somatic/visual channel. Further, each issue there presents cognitive phenomena absent or rare in spoken language.

9.1 Co-speech Gesture (I_1)

Gestures that accompany speech can be divided into two classes, those produced in association with a deictic and those produced otherwise—respectively "targeting" and "nontargeting" gestures.

9.1.1 Targeting Gestures (I_1a)

To begin with targeting gestures (T12 c5), the prototype of them is pointing, as when a speaker says *That's my horse* while aiming her straightened forefinger at the animal. This and all other types of targeting gestures share a property: the speaker's gesture is always at a different location than her target. The hearer/viewer accordingly must have a cognitive mechanism for spatially connecting the former with the latter.

One proposal for such a mechanism is that the hearer connects the gesture with the target by means of a cognitively generated "fictive chain". This chain is a succession of imaginal constructs—possibly from a relatively closed universal repertory—that are either schematic structures (largely geometric in character) or operations that affect such structures. Such a fictive chain may have three properties of a physical mechanical system: 1) It is fully connected without gaps. 2) It forms progressively from the gesture to the target, not in place all at once, nor from target to gesture. 3) It is causal: the gesture gives rise to the first fictive construct, the first construct to the second, and so on.

To illustrate such a fictive chain with the example just given, the pointing finger may first be schematized as a straight line with a front endpoint. This line then coaxially emits a straight one-dimensional intangible projection. The projection progresses quickly through space to intersect with and terminate at the horse. This intersection marks the horse as the intended target.

Numerous types of targeting gesture other than the prototype exist. We here select one of them to illustrate the range of the fictive chain. Thus, in referring to two glasses standing respectively ten and eleven feet in a straight line away from her, a speaker says *This glass is mine and that glass is yours*. She gestures by extending her arm toward the glasses with her flat hand held bent upward at the wrist, first orienting her palm and waving her fingers toward herself and then rotating her palm in the opposite direction and waving her fingers away from herself. The hearer may here generate a fictive chain in which an imaginal copy of the speaker's hand is first repositioned through space to a location between the two glasses. Then the initial waving motion of this fictive hand acts as a thrust that launches a fictive projection. This projection in turn progresses through space to intersect with the closer glass to mark it as the initial target. The fictive hand then rotates in synchrony with the actual articulator to launch a fictive projection at the further glass to mark it as the second target.

9.1.2   Nontargeting Gestures (I1b)
Co-speech gesturing not associated with a deictic includes body language, facial expressions, and different types of manual gestures (e.g., Kendon, 2004). Significantly, though, a semantic characteristic prevalent among the first two gestural categories as well as most manual types is that the meaning of the gestures—the conceptual content associated with them—is approximative, vague, or murky. For example, hunching may suggest only a rough sense of self-protection, and sweeping a hand with palm turned down away from oneself only a rough sense of not wanting.

By contrast, perhaps most spoken-language morphemes, especially those with segmental form, seem to be associated with concepts experienced as precise, crisp, and clear. This is the case even where the associated concept itself pertains to vagueness, like the word *amorphous*.

However, something of the approximative semantic character of much nontargeting gesturing does seem to occur in spoken language. Thus, among segmental morphemes, it may occur in some discourse-organizing forms like the *well* used to begin a sentence. It also seems to occur in English with certain bound Greco-Latin morphemes existing beside independent forms. For example, the termination *-cracy*—as in *democracy, autocracy, plutocracy, theocracy, technocracy*—seems to afford an approximate sense of 'rule of the government by', yet does not equal the clarity of this phrase. Even vaguer are the concepts associated with such nonsegmental morphemes as grammatical relations, like that of direct-object status, or alternatives of constituent order expressing subtly different patterns of emphasis.

Still, nontargeting gesturing may be the best arena in which to examine the cognitive phenomenon of conceptual vagueness.

9.2   *Signed Language (I2)*
Each signed language generally includes several distinct communication subsystems, but one of these is seemingly always the "classifier" subsystem—the focus of this section. This extensive subsystem is specialized for representing objects moving, located, or oriented with respect to each other in space and time (Emmorey, 2003).

This signed subsystem has several substantial differences from spoken language (T3, T13). These differences across two forms of human communication require an analysis of linguistic cognition far more general than that provided by extant analyses based on spoken language alone, and suggest an advance in language theory (T3 s4).

The comparison can begin with an illustration of the classifier subsystem. Within a single expression, it can represent an event in which a car drives quickly along a bumpy road that curves uphill closely past a tree, starting further away from the tree than it ends up. The signer's dominant hand represents the Figure—here in the classifier shape for a land vehicle; her nondominant hand represents the Ground—here in the classifier shape for a tree. The "vehicle" hand, "while oscillating" up and down, moves quickly across the chest and then along a curved path that ascends closely around the "tree" hand, stopping shortly past it.

The signed classifier subsystem differs from spoken language in at least the following three ways.

9.2.1   Number of Independent Parameters (I2a)

The signed classifier subsystem has many more independent parameters than spoken language does. The term "parameter" here designates any aspect of a communication system that can represent conceptual content independently of other such aspects. Then spoken language has basically three such parameters—phonetic quality, pitch, and loudness. But by one count, the signed classifier subsystem has some thirty parameters (T13). In the example, for instance, these parameters include the shape of the Figure hand, the shape of the Ground hand, the Figure hands' speed, its self-referencing motion (here, oscillatory), the contour of its path (here, curved), the vertical angle of its path (here, partly upward), the distance of its path from the Ground (here, close), and the relative lengths of its path segments before and after encounter with the Ground. As parameters, all these aspects of the classifier subsystem can vary independently of each other.

9.2.2   Scene Partitioning (I2b)

The classifier subsystem seems generally closer to visual perception than spoken language does in its partitioning of a scene. Thus, in our example, it is the same single element, the dominant hand, that represents the Figure's identity, oscillation, and path, including the path's speed, contour, vertical angle, and relation to the Ground. That is, the classifier subsystem clusters together those aspects of the situation that are associated with the Figure. It separates off only the non-Figure-related aspects—the Ground's identity and location—for representation by the nondominant hand. This scene partitioning presumably resembles visual scene parsing.

By contrast, every spoken language deviates from such perceptual fidelity. Thus, one English sentence that captures the same concepts represented by the classifier expression might be: *The car bumped quickly up a road that wound closely around a tree, starting further away than it ended up.* The arrangement of the concepts in this sentence's phrases and constructions has little similarity to that of their visual counterparts.

9.2.3   Iconicity (I2c)
The signed classifier subsystem exhibits far more iconicity than spoken language does. In iconicity, linguistic form represents conceptual content through similarity with it. An example of it in spoken language is seen in *The cell phone tower is waay / waaaay / waaaaaay over there*. Here, the successive increases in the length of the vowel over the norm in way represent corresponding increases in the length of the tower's displacement from the speaker that simple way would have indicated. However, such instances of iconicity in spoken language are rare.

But of the thirty some parameters in the classifier system, all are iconic except the two for the Figure and Ground identities, of which only some are iconic. For example, the characteristics of the Figure hand's path—its speed, contour, vertical angle, and relation to the Ground—are iconic of the same characteristics of the path exhibited by the actual Figure object. Further, these parameters largely reflect the gradience of what they represent, unlike the preestablished discrete values of the structure-indicating elements of spoken language.

10   Relations across Cognitive Faculties (J)

Language is often approached as a self-contained cognitive faculty, one with its own specifically linguistic elements of organization, generally independent of other faculties in cognition. But by the analysis here, language shares parts of its organization with other cognitive faculties and could not function without their participation.

To begin with some theoretical background, cognition can be provisionally divided into different "faculties" of greater or lesser extent, each judged to perform some integrated function. And a faculty can be judged to behave either more as a medium that is organized, a "cognitive system", or more as the organization of a medium, a "cognitive organizer".[11] Here, organizing is meant to

---

11   The term "system" is here used over "module" (Fodor, 1983) because, unlike the autonomy ascribed to modules, systems regularly share cognitive organizers and interact with each other.

cover both static structures and dynamic processes. Language in particular is here treated as a cognitive system.

Major cognitive systems appear to have evolved at different times in phylogenesis. Presumably among the earliest were motor control and perception in general or in its various modalities, including the chemical, tactile, visual, and auditory. Later evolving systems may have included affect and ideation (having and manipulating ideas). And cognitive systems that seem to have evolved in the lineage leading to humans—whether anew or from a prior more elementary form—include language, gesture, music, dance, art, and culture. Seemingly also co-evolving with these were much elaborated forms of affect and ideation (including intellective processes like imagining, inferring, and reasoning).

Cognitive organizers, in turn, might be grouped into three types. "Structural" organizers include structuring in general as well as particular forms of it such as spatial, temporal, causal, categorial, combinatorial, and analogic. "Cognizing" organizers include (the patterning and processing provided by) attention, memory, learning, and epistemology. And "constitutive" organizers include (the degree to which a cognitive system manifests) intensity, elaboration, plasticity, and consistency. As noted, some of these cognitive organizers (e.g., attention) could alternatively be treated as cognitive systems.

Language can be related to other cognitive systems or to cognitive organizers both externally and internally, as addressed next in order.

10.1   *Language's External Relations to Other Cognitive Systems (J1)*

The external relations of language to other cognitive systems include a comparison of the cognitive organizers relevant to it versus to them. A given cognitive organizer can occur in just one, some, or all cognitive systems. Accordingly, cognitive systems can share particular cognitive organizers in what (T9) calls the "overlapping systems model of cognitive organization". The comparison can indicate how cognitive systems might be alike or different and hence how they might relate to each other evolutionarily. The next two sections look at cognitive organizers that language respectively does not and does share with other cognitive systems. Evidence for organization in language is here based wholly on its closed-class morphemes, since these underlie one of its most fundamental structuring mechanisms [4.1] (T1 c1).

10.1.1   Noncommonality of Organization (J1a)

A comparison of language with any other major cognitive system generally shows that certain cognitive organizers are prominent in one while minimal in the other, in both directions. Such a comparison is proposed next for language and visual perception (T9).

10.1.1.1 *Prominent in Language Organization, Minimal in Visual Organization (J1a1)*

Prominent in language but only minimal in visual perception are two categories within the cognitive organizer of epistemology. These two are (the judgment of) reality status and evidentiality—addressed next in order.

Reality Status. Seemingly all languages have closed-class—hence, structural—representation of reality status [4.1.6]. For example, the conceptual content represented by a sentence can be designated as actual (*I danced*), negative (*I didn't dance*), counterfactual (*I should have danced*), potential (*I might dance*), or conditional (*I would dance if I had the time*).

Though requiring empirical confirmation, it can be conjectured that visual perception by contrast lacks a range of ways to interpret the reality status of a scene. It seems that, when viewed, a scene is simply taken to be actual.

Evidentiality. Perhaps all languages have closed-class representation of evidentiality—whether the speaker takes the sentence's proposition as factual or infers it as probable (*He is home now / must be home by now*) [4.1.6 (D1f3)]. Some languages obligatorily mark this judgment and, with regard to inference, distinguish several types of it. For example, they might direct a hearer to infer the occurrence of an event based on its consequences; its periodicity of occurrence; the nonvisual stimuli it produces; or reports about it. Thus, if the Atsugewi consequence evidential *-it'* is suffixed to the verb root *am-* 'eat', the result can express the likelihood that people were eating at a table on the evidence of dirty dishes there.

Though again needing experimentation, visual perception by contrast seemingly does not mark elements within a scene for their evidentiary status but rather represents them as they appear or in accord with expectation. To illustrate the latter, the visual system does not flag an occluded portion of a configuration—say, the portion of a molding located behind a cabinet—as being 'unknown' or 'inferred as present'. Rather, the perceptual system generally "fills it in" unconsciously with the expected characteristics. In effect, such conformance with expectation is "antievidential".

10.1.1.2 *Prominent in Visual Organization, Minimal in Language Organization (J1a2)*

The opposite balance—minimal in language but prominent in visual perception—is seen within another cognitive organizer, spatial organization, for two of its categories: rotation and dilation.

Rotation. Some languages, including English, have closed-class representation of rotation. But these mostly mark only one structural aspect of rotation, the orientation of the spin axis and, within that aspect, they distinguish only vertical and horizontal, as seen respectively in *I turned the bucket around / over*.

By contrast, visual perception can apparently represent diverse structural aspects of rotation with some granularity. Thus, a viewer can perceive many different orientations of spin axis, as of a baton twirled around at various angles. A viewer can also perceive certain different geometric relations that the spin axis has to the rotating object: at the object's center—e.g., a disk spinning around; at its endpoint—e.g., an arm swinging around; and outside it—e.g., a squirrel running around a tree trunk. As the examples just cited show, English here can only use *around* for all three cases. And, for this third case, a viewer can further perceive different extents of rotation—from part of a circuit, to one complete circuit, to a few circuits, to many circuits. English can again use only *around* while structurally indicating different extents only indirectly by inference from different temporal constructions, as in *I ran around the house for 20 seconds / in one minute / for five minutes / for hours*.

Dilation. Some languages, including English, have closed-class representation of "dilation". But these mostly mark only two structural aspects of it: its sign, that is, contraction vs. expansion, and number, whether one or more objects engage in it. Thus, English represents contraction vs. expansion for a single object with *in* and *out* (*The large air bladder suddenly snapped in / out*) and for plural objects with *together* and *apart* (*The ball bearings all rolled together / apart*).

Contrast this with visual perception. To be sure, within a viewed scene, a dilation's sign and number can certainly be visually perceived. But a viewer can also perceive further structural aspects. One is the dimensional number of a single dilating object, like expansion in the one, two, or three dimensions of a bungee cord stretching out, an oil slick spreading out, or dough puffing out—all of which English uses *out* to represent without further differentiation. A viewer can additionally perceive whether dilation involves a solid entity or only a perimeter, as with expansion in a rubber sheet vs. a rubber band stretching out, or in dough vs. a transparent balloon puffing out. Again, English here only uses *out*. And vision can perceive whether or not an object's apparent contraction or expansion is due to an increase or decrease in the distance between it and a viewer—a structural category unrecognized in language.

10.1.2   Commonality of Organization (J1b)
Complementarily to the preceding differences, language shares some cognitive organizers with every other cognitive system. In the next three subsections, we address such commonalities between language and visual perception, ideation, and the cognitive systems that co-evolved with language in the lineage leading to humans (T9).

10.1.2.1   *Commonalities of Organization between Language and Vision (J1b1)*
While [10.1.1] addressed differences in organization between language and visual perception, we here address commonalities. One such commonality may occur in "spatial schematization", which includes conformation and topology, addressed next in order.

Conformation. Perhaps every language has closed-class forms representing some geometric-type spatial properties of a Figure object's site or path relative to a Ground object, termed "conformation" in (T4). For one English site example, the preposition *in*, as in *The large rock (F) is in the fish tank (G)*, indicates that the Ground can be conceptually schematized as a plane so curved as to define a volume of space, and that the Figure occupies a portion of that volume.

Though needing experimental confirmation, a viewer, on perceiving the rock and the tank, may well also perceive the rock as occupying a portion of the space enclosed by the tank. That is, she may visually perceive a structural relation of an 'in' type of conformation.

Topology. Topology is a geometric abstraction that disregards specific Euclidean form. To use *in* again for illustration, this preposition is in fact neutral to several aspects of such form. As already seen in [4.1.1 (D1a1)], it is neutral to magnitude—(*a pill*) *in a thimble* / (*lava*) *in a volcano*; to shape—*in a well* / *trench*); to continuity—*in a bell jar* / *bird cage*; and to closure—*in a beach ball* / *punch bowl*.

But it can be conjectured that visual processing—beside a Euclidean representation specific to form—also produces a topological representation, so that a viewer of the eight scenes just represented linguistically would also perceive an abstract visual representation consisting simply of one object included in or surrounded by another.

10.1.2.2   *Commonalities of Organization between Language and Ideation (J1b2)*
We posit that, in evolving, the cognitive system of ideation has come to include a subsystem of "explanation". This subsystem generates mental models that are experienced as accounting for the structure and function of some domain of phenomena in terms of concepts already accepted. An explanation can range over various levels of consistency, elaboration, and sophistication.

Linguistic closed-class concepts seem to have much overlap with concepts in certain less sophisticated types of explanation, and may have been the model for them. Such less sophisticated types include naive personal accounts, traditional cultural lore, casual science, and early science.

We next present two possible examples of such overlap, selected from the eight examples detailed in (T9).

Linguistic Fictive Sensory Paths and the Extramission Theory of Perception. Many languages can represent an event of perception as a "sensory path"—one type of fictive motion (motion conceptualized but unperceived [4.1.1 (D1a1)]). Where the perceiver initiates the event agentively, the direction of this path is generally conceived as going from the perceiver to the perceived entity. For the visual modality, English can represent this circumstance with the verb *look* as in *I looked down into the valley*. It has no construction in the "perceived-to-perceiver" direction, say, something like **The valley "looked" up out to me*.

But this linguistic bias matches the "extramission" theory of vision, in which the eyes emit beams that project through the air until they contact the perceived object. This theory was held by the early science of classical Greece and persists today as the naive view of up to fifty percent of adults (Winer and Cottrell, 1996). Modern sophisticated science has replaced this conception of vision with the "intromission" theory of photons proceeding from an object to the eye.

Linguistic Force Dynamics and the Early Impetus Theory of Motion. In one basic pattern of force dynamics (T1 c7) [4.1.4]—the extended causing of motion—a moving entity's tendency toward rest is overcome by a stronger external entity and so continues moving, as seen in *The ball rolled on because of the wind blowing on it*. Correspondingly, the medieval theory of impetus continued Aristotle's view that a moving object will intrinsically come to rest unless some external force keeps it in motion. By contrast, modern physics holds that an object has no internal tendency toward a particular state of motion but continues at its current velocity unless affected externally.

10.1.2.3 *Commonalities of Organization across Language and the Other Human-Lineage Cognitive Systems (J1b3)*

Language and the other five cognitive systems cited above that appeared in the lineage leading to humans share particular forms of certain cognitive organizers. Specifically, all these cognitive systems exhibit "combinatorial structure" and "group-level organization", addressed next in order. These systems may share those two forms because they co-evolved with language or evolved later partly modeled on it. This is a focal area in which organizational relations across faculties have implications for the evolutionary relations among those faculties(T9).

Combinatorial Structure. Language seems to be the human cognitive system with the most combinatorial structure, exhibiting numerous forms of it across many subsystems and levels, as detailed in [5]. As seen there, it appears for example in the combination of phonetic features into phonemes, phonemes into morphemes, morphemes into multimorphemic words, single- and multi-morphemic words into phrases, phrases into clauses, clauses into multi-clausal sentences, single- and multi-clausal sentences into single-speaker turns, and such turns into dialogs.

But many forms of combinatorial structure appear as well in the other five late-evolving human systems. The cognitive system of music, for example, can be analyzed as having at least the following three types of combining. In one type, there is an inventory consisting of the notes of a scale or "pitch set", and each instantiation includes a selection of those notes arranged consecutively in accord with rules of tonal sequencing. Another type of combination has an inventory consisting of distinct temporal lengths, and each instantiation includes a selection of such durations assigned consecutively to each note and each inter-note interval in accord with rules of rhythmic organization. And the third type has an inventory consisting of distinct degrees of emphasis or intensity, and each instantiation includes a selection of such accenting for assignment to the notes in accord with rules of pulse or beat patterning. When these three types of combination are themselves combined, the result is an emergent higher-level unit, a melody.

Group-Level Organization. Pre-human cognitive systems are largely invariant across a whole species. For example, across the entire species of bald eagles, cognitive systems generally consistent in their operation include visual perception and motor control, for example, as these relate to flight. The same holds for the cognitive system of communication across vervet monkeys (a more elementary precursor of language) (Seyfarth and Cheney, 2012).

But a different form of organization appears in all the cognitive systems arising in the human lineage, and this new form itself had to have arisen through evolution. While on the one hand these systems do each have certain aspects of organization in common across the human species, they also exhibit distinct patterns of organization across different geographically or socially based groups. This is "group-level organization", here assigned to the constitutive cognitive organizer of plasticity.

Thus, beside linguistic universals, distinct languages exist that can differ extensively in their phonology, morphology, syntax, semantics, and lexicons. Such group-level differences—again beside certain pan-human structural commonalities—are also present in the cognitive systems that co-evolved with language, including culture, gesture, music, dance, and art. Certain disciplines have formed specifically to analyze such group-level differences in these cognitive systems, such as anthropology for culture and ethnomusicology for music.[12]

10.2 Language's Internal Relations to Other Cognitive Faculties (J2)

While the preceding section [J1] addressed language's external relations with other cognitive systems—how it resembles or differs from them in organization—the present section addresses how language directly engages other cognitive faculties, both cognitive systems and cognitive organizers, in its "internal" relations with them. More specifically, language can function as an interface between a number of faculties (or between particular components or applications of such faculties). It coordinates them and integrates their functions and can associate them in an established lexicon as well as in novel expressions.

To be sure, attention has been directed, especially in the psychological literature, to various respects in which other cognitive faculties relate to and play a role in the use of language. But the present section may be the first attempt to directly address such relations and roles in their collectivity as part of the intrinsic organization of language and as an issue in its own right. The following four subsections address different aspects of such internal faculty relations in language.

10.2.1 Faculties Underlying Morphemes (J2a)

In nearly every morpheme of any language's lexicon, there is an association of the cognitive faculties that underlie language's three main divisions of form, meaning, and grammar [1]. What underlies form is the cognitive organizer of structuring. Specifically, this is the structuring of a phonological representation, which organizes the cognitive systems of motor control for vocalization in the speaker and of auditory perception in the hearer. What underlies meaning are the cognitive systems of ideation and affect (here equally designated as "conceptual"). And underlying the formal aspect of grammar are certain structural cognitive organizers such as categoriality, while underlying its semantic aspect are the same faculties just cited as underlying meaning. In any given morpheme, then, all these faculties are associated with each other.

---

[12] The Sapir-Whorf hypothesis, in proposing a conceptual alignment between a language's grammar and the speaker's culture, makes sense only under an assumption of group-level variation.

We can use the English morpheme spelled *puny* to illustrate this association across faculties, particularized for that morpheme. The morpheme's form is underlain by the cognitive organizer of structuring, particularized as the phonological representation /pyuni/ as well as by the two cognitive systems in play in a speaker's sequential motoric production of the sounds and a hearer's auditory perception of them. In turn, the morpheme's meaning is underlain by the cognitive systems of ideation with its particular concept 'small in size' and of affect with its particular attitude 'derogation'. The formal aspect of the morpheme's grammar is underlain by the cognitive organizer of categoriality, particularized as the lexical category "adjective". And the semantic aspect of the morpheme's grammar is underlain by the cognitive system of ideation, particularized as the concept 'attribute'. All these faculties and their particularizations are put in association by the morpheme.

10.2.2 Faculties Underlying Extended Communication (J2b)
An association of the faculties underlying form, meaning, and grammar similar to that just seen for individual morphemes continues when morphemes are combined into expressions, as in *That horse won the race*. But such expressional meaning can be extended in what might be viewed as an expanding sphere of communication, first by gesture and then by context, as addressed next in order.

10.2.2.1 *Gesture (J2b1)*
Spoken language is often accompanied by co-speech gesture [9.1]. Such gesture expresses semantic content about the same topic that the verbal content is about, but often different from that verbal content. This gestural meaning is underlain as in the verbal case by the cognitive systems of ideation and affect. But it also requires the integration of further cognitive faculties. Four cases of such additions are addressed next.

First, a gesture requires additional motor control by the speaker—now not of the vocal apparatus but of other parts of the body—and, newly here, visual perception by the hearer, specifically of those parts of the speaker's body.

To illustrate with an example from Beattie and Shovelton (1999), while describing a comic book story involving a vintage car, the respondent says *So the hand is now trying to start the car* and gestures by circling in the air with his hand as if winding a crank. The hearer here visually perceives the speaker's bodily movement and integrates its distinct conceptual content with the verbal content.

Second, if the gesture is of the targeting type [9.1.1], the hearer must extend his visual perception from the speaker's body alone to the environmental surroundings. For example, a speaker entering an airport with a companion might say *That's my father* and gesture by pointing a finger at a particular man some distance away there. To interpret the speaker's utterance, the hearer must regard not only the speaker's gesture but also the man in the environment as well as how both the gesture and the man are situated within that environment.

Note that while some deictics *can* be accompanied by a targeting gesture, others require one. English examples are *thataway* and *yay*, as in *The gunman rode off thataway* and *The fish I caught was yay big*—said while gesturally indicating respectively a direction and a linear extent (T12 c5). This observation is significant in that a morpheme can be lexicalized to associate together the faculties underlying not only the usual form, meaning, and grammar but also gesture.

Third, in viewing a targeting gesture, the hearer cognitively constructs a "fictive chain" of imaginal elements progressing through space from the gesture to the targeted object [9.1.1]. In the preceding "airport" example, this can consist of the hearer imagining the speaker's extended finger as coaxially emitting a fictive linear projection that progresses rapidly through space until it intersects with and stops at the distal object to mark it as the speaker's intended target. Such a fictive chain generated in the hearer's cognition involves the cognitive system of visual perception, as does gesture itself. But unlike gesture, it is attenuated under the cognitive organizer of intensity to function at the "Semi-Abstract Level of Palpability" (T1 c2).

Fourth, a gesture can require the integration of yet another cognitive faculty, the cognitive organizer of analogy. For example, after saying *My sister in Dublin has a tattoo*, a speaker might add *right here* and gesture by placing her right palm onto her left shoulder. In addition to bringing in the cognitive systems of motor control in the speaker and perception in the hearer, this gesture initiates in the hearer's cognition an analogical mapping of the tattoo's location from the speaker's left shoulder to that of the cognitive representation expressed by the subject NP (T12 c14).

10.2.2.2 Context (*J2b2*)

The context [4.5] of an expression and any gesture accompanying it can affect their meaning. And such context can require certain applications of particular cognitive faculties. It might, for example, require visual perception of the physical surroundings, knowledge (< epistemology) of the culture, and memory of the interlocutors' history.

For example, if in a restaurant one family member says to another *Don't lick the knife this time*, the appropriate interpretation of the sentence by those present rests contextually on their visually identifying the relevant knife in the addressee's hand, knowing that licking one's knife in public is inappropriate in their culture, and remembering that the addressee had done this in the past.

10.2.3   Faculties Underlying Certain Semantic Distinctions (J2c)

It can be posited that particular cognitive faculties are responsible for certain semantic distinctions present in language. Proposed next are four such distinctions and the faculties underlying them.

10.2.3.1   *Factivity (J2c1)*

Every morpheme or sensible expression has what can be called a "conceptual representation". This is the conceptual content that, to take the hearer's perspective, is evoked in his cognition on hearing the form. But in a speaker's or hearer's belief system, a conceptual representation can exhibit a particular distinction. It can be held either to correspond or not correspond to something in reality—respectively a "factive representation" and a "fictive representation". The cognitive organizer of epistemology has a component of "factivity" responsible for ascribing actuality or nonactuality to a conceptual representation.

To illustrate this distinction for morphemes, both *bucket* and *dragon* equally evoke a conceptual representation in a hearer when they are uttered—a representation that here can include a vivid image. But these conceptual representations likely engage the hearer's epistemological faculty and further evoke a sense of being respectively existent and nonexistent as factive and fictive representations.

And to illustrate this distinction for expressions, the subjects of *My sister in Dublin has a tattoo* and of *The hero in my novel has a tattoo* both have a conceptual representation—that of a person. But a hearer would likely judge these representations to be respectively factive and fictive.

10.2.3.2   *Specificity (J2c2)*

Under a linguistic distinction of "specificity", a conceptual representation can be either specific or nonspecific. That is, it has either a particular instantiation or only a generic or potential realization.

This distinction can be seen in a factive conceptual representation like *A lawyer approached me* vs. *I needed to find a lawyer*. It can also be seen in a fictive conceptual representation, as in a fantasy novel, like *A dragon approached me* vs. *I went in search of a dragon*.

10.2.3.3   *Access (J2c3)*

A conceptual representation that is both factive and specific is commonly called a "direct referent" in linguistics and philosophy. But such a direct referent can exhibit a further distinction that might be called "access"—it is either physically accessible or inaccessible. In the case of accessibility, a speaker or hearer can currently perceive it or motorically act on it—operations of the cognitive systems of perception and motor control—whereas in the case of inaccessibility they cannot.

To illustrate, the subject of the earlier example *My sister in Dublin has a tattoo* has a direct referent, but one that is inaccessible to the speaker and hearer. However, the subject of *The man across the room has a tattoo* has a direct referent that *is* accessible to them. And the hearer integrates this accessibility into the meaning of the expression.

Note that a speaker can add the earlier-seen phrase *right here* and hand-on-shoulder gesture to any of the three "tattoo" sentences, showing that analogical mapping can be applied to an object whether it is accessibly factive, inaccessibly factive, or fictive.

Some further characteristics of access can be cited. First, direct reference to the accessible and to the inaccessible can be juxtaposed—the transition often drawing little attention—as where a speaker in Berkeley says *The chef here is slicing a parsnip that was grown in Bristol*. Further, conceptual representation of the inaccessible can continue indefinitely in a "story world" (Costello et al., 1995) with its own "internal timeline" (T12). And reference to the inaccessible can be conducted even amidst a welter of currently accessible perceptions, as when two speakers discuss a topic while walking down a busy street.

10.2.3.4 Targeting (J2c4)

A linguistic trigger points to a target that can be either deictic or anaphoric [1.4]. That is, the target can be in the physical environment extending out from the speaker and hearer or in the current discourse between them. These alternatives are underlain by partly distinct cognitive faculties.

The iPhone example in [1.4] can be used here again. When the speaker says *That's the new iPhone* and points to an object in a display case, the deictic trigger *that* directs the hearer to coordinate the cognitive systems of ideation and structuring, which underlie the expression's meaning, with the cognitive system of visual perception, which underlies his current viewing of the gesture and of the object within their environment. But when the speaker says *The new iPhone is out—that's what I'd like for Christmas*, the anaphoric trigger *that*—though again invoking the cognitive systems that underlie the expression's meaning—now directs the hearer to coordinate those with the cognitive organizer of memory: his working memory of the previously uttered nominal and its meaning.

10.2.4 Limitations on Faculty Coordination (J2d)

The coordination that language carries out across faculties can be great, as in the cases above, but it also has limitations. We next look at three areas, each with sectors that do and sectors that do not (or only minimally) coordinate faculties. These contrasts in faculty participation can help sharpen the contours of language's coordinating role.

10.2.4.1   *The Sapir-Whorf Hypothesis (J2d1)*

The Sapir-Whorf hypothesis (e.g., Whorf, 1956) proposes a strong alignment between the conceptual organization of a language's grammar and that of the speakers' thought and culture. In terms of faculties, the proposal is that ideation and affect (cognitive systems) exhibit a similar structuring (a cognitive organizer) on the one hand in the semantic aspect of a language's grammar and, on the other hand, in both the thought and the culture (cognitive systems) of the language's speakers.

Evidence for a grammar-thought alignment is relatively ample. For example, speakers of a verb-framed language without ready syntactic means for representing Manner evidently tend not to include Manner in their thoughts about a Figure's motion or to take note of it in an observed situation (Slobin, 2006).

But evidence for a grammar-culture alignment is quite slight. For example, kinship relations and totemic affiliations have great cultural elaboration and attention in Aboriginal Australia (Heath et al., 1982). But the language of the Mparntwe Arrernte there (Wilkins, 1993) may have only one fully explicit grammatical reflection of such attention. Specifically, there are distinct personal pronouns for plural referents with certain kinship relations. But this is minute relative to the entire grammatical system of the language (T2 c8).

10.2.4.2   *Embodiment (J2d2)*

As used in linguistics, embodiment is generally the idea that the semantic organization of a language as well as speakers' understanding of expressions in it, whether concrete or abstract, are largely based on the speakers' experience with their own perception and bodily action. The idea hence posits a coordination between two sets of faculties. The first set consists of the cognitive systems of ideation and affect underlying linguistic meaning, while the second consists of the cognitive systems of perception and motor control.

But of the areas where embodiment might be expected to appear, some seem to show it extensively while others only slightly (T8). Two such areas, respectively, might be the meanings of open-class as against closed-class morphemes.

Thus, the meanings of many open-class morphemes seem to accord with a partitioning of the phenomenal continuum consistent with how the human body interacts with other physical phenomena—what might be called its "bulk encounter" with them. The human body is here understood in terms of its particular mesoscopic size and anatomy, as well as its possible actions and perceptions. Examples of such morphemes might be the nouns *hand, tree, star,* and the verbs *grab, run, look.* (The capacity for languages to differ here as well, though, is addressed in [7.4.1]).

But the meanings of many closed-class forms are topological in character—neutral to such Euclidean specifics as size, contour, and angle [10.1.2 (J1b1)]—and so do not accord with bulk encounter. If bulk encounter mattered here, it should help determine how physical phenomena are categorized linguistically. Yet this seems rarely the case.

For example, the English preposition *along* requires that the Ground be schematizable as linear and that the Figure execute a linear path adjacent to it. But, as seen in *The ant climbed up along the matchstick* and *The squirrel climbed up along the tree trunk*, the Ground object can be of any size—it is magnitude neutral. Now, one's body will encounter these two Ground objects—a matchstick and a tree trunk—quite differently. Yet the preposition, by abstracting out their common geometric feature of linearity, groups them together—contrary to bulk-encounter notions of embodiment.

Comparably, the preposition *across* requires that the Ground be schematizable as a horizontal planar strip and that the Figure execute a path from one edge perpendicularly to the opposite edge of the strip. But, as seen in *The bug crawled across my palm* and *The bus drove across the country*, the Path and Ground are again magnitude neutral. Yet one's body encounters a hand's breadth and a cross-country span quite differently. Again, the morpheme's abstractive topological schema trumps Euclidean bodily specifics.

10.2.4.3   Iconicity (J2d3)

Iconicity in language occurs where linguistic form represents meaning through similarity with it [9.2]. In terms of cognitive faculties, the structuring (a cognitive organizer) of an expression's form is similar to the structuring exhibited by the ideation or affect (cognitive systems) represented by its meaning.

To illustrate, the increased length of the vowel in *waaay* as in *The cell tower is waaay over there* is similar to and thereby represents an increased length in the tower's remove above what simple *way* would have indicated. Or again, the sequence of the verbs in *We arrived, ate, and left* is the same as and so represents the sequence in which their referents took place. And the sound of the noun *caw* is judged to resemble and thereby to help represent the call of a crow—an instance of onomatopoeia.

But there are also opportunities for iconicity that are rarely used (T13). For example, the rate of a Figure's Motion, from stationary to slow to fast, is seldom represented by the rate of speech, from slow to moderate to fast, as suggested in (12a) respectively by spaced lettering, ordinary lettering, and italics. And pauses between events are seldom represented by pauses between the phrases expressing those events, as suggested in (12b) by sequences of dots.

(12) a. T h e p e n l a y o n t h e t a b l e, rolled to the edge, *and fell down*.
 b. He entered .... sat down .... and pulled out her letter.

11   Research Characteristics (K)

Every study on conceptual structure in language is shaped by the methodologies and other aspects of approach used in the research—two features discussed next in order.

11.1   *Methodology (K1)*

Linguistic meaning is amenable to study through a range of methodologies, that is, one or another system of procedures used to examine it (T5). Each methodology has a different profile of capacities and limitations that accords it a particular perspective on the nature of conceptual organization in language. Together, they thus afford an array of advantages and compensate for each other's deficits.

Used in conjunction with all of these is one "meta-methodology", analytic thought, which includes abstraction, comparison, correlation, classification, pattern detection, inference, and in general the systematic manipulation of ideas. In addition, we next enumerate some of the main methodologies used to research linguistic conceptual structure.

The traditional and still most prevalent methodology in cognitive semantics is metacognition. This is the use of directed conscious attention to introspectively accessed aspects of language in one's own cognition. Such metacognition plays a role at three levels of remove. At the most immediate, a linguist examines her own native language. At the second, a linguist elicits and examines reports by others using introspection on their native language, as a descriptive linguist does with native speakers. At the third level, a linguist examines written descriptions by other linguists of their work with native speakers, as a typologist does with the grammars of different languages.

Another methodology is corpus research, the largely computer-aided examination of representative and often annotated collections of portions of writing or spontaneous speech. Yet another is the analysis of audio- and videographic recordings of naturally occurring communication. Still others are the experimental techniques of psycholinguistics; the instrumental probes of the brain's linguistic functioning in neuroscience; and the simulations of human linguistic functions in artificial intelligence.

Some comparison of the profiles of these methodologies can suggest where they excel and where they offset each other's limitations. What metacognition seems best at is determining certain types of meaning. These are mainly the concepts associated with individual open-class segmental morphemes, idioms, and tropes, as well as whole utterances and interchanges. As a consciousness phenomenon, metacognition may in fact be the only methodology able to access meaning, another consciousness phenomenon.

Metacognition also excels at determining whether an utterance is well-formed semantically and syntactically, the latter being the basis of grammaticality judgments.

At a somewhat lower level, metacognition has partial but not thoroughgoing access to cross-morphemic relations in the lexicon [4.2.2 (D2b3)]. Thus, regarding access to synonymy, if asked to think of other words with roughly the same meaning as, say, *tendency*, a respondent might come up with a couple, but probably not all, of the following: *inclination, leaning, disposition, proneness, propensity*, and *proclivity*. And regarding access to a morpheme's polysemous range, a speaker asked to identify the various senses of the noun *stock* might come up with several, but scarcely all, of those listed in [7.4.3]. However, this metacognitive deficit can be compensated for by lexicography—a methodology akin to corpus research that collates dispersed occurrences of particular forms and meanings—in the form of dictionaries and thesauruses, respectively.

Perhaps still less accessible through metacognition are the particular forms and conceptual import of certain concomitants of speech—auditory ones like vocal dynamics and intonation and visual ones like gesture, facial expression, and body language. But this introspective shortfall can be made up for through the methodology of audiovisual recording and its subsequent analysis.

And perhaps even more inaccessible to introspection are the bases, whether purely formal or also partly semantic, of certain syntactic effects. For example, if asked to consider the two sentences *Whose dog did our cat bite?* and *Whose dog bit our cat?*, an average speaker would have little direct sense for what it is about the first sentence that requires the inclusion of the word *did*, the basic form of the verb *bite*, and the positioning of this verb at the sentence's end, while the second sentence requires an absence of *did*, the past-tense form of the verb, and the positioning of the verb within the sentence. In compensation for this introspective deficiency, however, syntacticians combine their metacognitive access to whether a sentence is well- or ill-formed with the meta-methodology of analytic thought to uncover the underlying patterns.

And at the lowest level, some aspects of linguistically represented meaning are entirely inaccessible to metacognition and rely wholly on other methodologies for any understanding of them. Thus, there is no introspective access to the cognitive processing of meaning that takes place in fractions of a second nor that occurs across different individuals. But the techniques of psycholinguistics can access that time scale and can compare the performances of different individuals on a particular semantic function. Metacognition can also not access which brain systems are involved in different types of semantic processing, but that lack is partly made up for by neuroscientific imaging techniques. And there can be no direct metacognitive access to methods for processing linguistically represented conceptual content other than those actually present in cognition, whereas artificial intelligence, aided by the meta-methodology of analytic thought, has developed just such methods.

11.2 Other Aspects of Approach (K2)

In addition to the methodologies used, studies in cognitive semantics can differ with respect to certain structural research parameters. To briefly identify four of these, one parameter is scope, ranging from a larger swath to a more focused area under examination. Another parameter, that of granularity, tends to correlate inversely with that of scope, ranging from an analysis in broader strokes for a larger scope to one in finer detail for a smaller scope.

Another parameter involves a study's balance between the theoretical and the descriptive. And yet another parameter involves a balance between the introduction of new ideas and the elaboration of familiar ideas.

Conclusion

Language, we posit, evolved among hominins as a system by which sentient individuals could volitionally communicate to each other a broad range of conceptual content—both ideation and affect—with some specificity and speed. Within cognition, it is a cognitive system whose characteristics are in part unique to that system, in part shared by some other cognitive systems, and in part the same across all cognitive systems in an "overlapping systems" model of cognitive organization.

Seemingly more than other cognitive systems, language is combinatorial in structure, with smaller units combining to form larger units in accord with rules. Further, unlike older cognitive systems but like those arising in the human lineage, language has group-level organization. Under it, individual "languages" form that can differ across different geographically or socially based groups. Linguistic characteristics can then be in common across all individual languages as universals, fall into a relatively small number of categories as a typology, fall into relatively numerous categories as a repertory, or differ across individual languages.

Language has a set of mechanisms that introduce structure into conceptual content or represent it there—the central concern of cognitive semantics. Through these and additional mechanisms, language may offer readier access to certain aspects of cognition in general than other cognitive systems do and so have an essential function within research in cognitive science, that is, in how the mind works.

References*

Baldrick, Chris. 2008. *Oxford Dictionary of Literary Terms*. New York: Oxford University Press.

Beattie, Geoffrey, and Heather Shovelton. 1999. Mapping the range of information contained in the iconic hand gestures that accompany spontaneous speech. *Journal of Language and Social Psychology*, 18(4), 438–462.

Bernstein, Basil. 1964. Elaborated and restricted codes: Their social origins and some consequences. *American Anthropologist* 66(6): 55–69.

Boroditsky, Lera, Lauren A. Schmidt, and Webb Phillips. 2003. Sex, syntax, and semantics. In D. Gentner and S. Goldin-Meadow (eds.), *Language in Mind: Advances in the Investigation of Language and Thought*, 157–191. Cambridge, MA: MIT Press.

Brugmann, Claudia and George Lakoff. 1988. Cognitive topology and lexical networks. In S. Small, G. Cottrell, and M. Tanenhaus (eds.), *Lexical Ambiguity Resolution: Perspectives from Psycholinguistics, Neuropsychology, and Artificial Intelligence*, 477–508. Menlo Park: Morgan Kaufmann.

Bybee, Joan. 2014. Cognitive processes in grammaticalization. In M. Tomasello (ed.), *The New Psychology of Language: Cognitive and Functional Approaches to Language Structure*, Volume II, 145–167. Mahwah: Lawrence Erlbaum.

Clark, Eve V. 1997. Conceptual perspective and lexical choice in acquisition. *Cognition* 64(1): 1–37.

Clark, Herbert H., and Susan E. Brennan. 1991. Grounding in communication. In L.B. Resnick, J.M. Levine, and S.D. Teasley (eds.), *Perspectives on Socially Shared Cognition*, 127–149. Washington: APA Books.

Costello, Anne M., Gail A. Bruder, Carol Hosenfeld, and Judith F. Duchan. 1995. A structural analysis of a fictional narrative: "A Free Night" by Anne Maury Costello.

---

* Almost all works by Leonard Talmy cited here are available on his website: https://www.acsu.buffalo.edu/~talmy/talmy.html.

In J.F. Duchan, G.A. Bruder, and L.E. Hewitt (eds.), *Deixis in Narrative: A Cognitive Science Perspective*, 461–466. Mahwah, NJ: Lawrence Erlbaum Associates, Inc.

Emmorey, Karen. 2003. *Language, Cognition, and the Brain: Insights from Sign Language Research*. Mahwah: Lawrence Erlbaum.

Fauconnier, Gilles and Mark B. Turner. 1996. Blending as a Central Process of Grammar. In A. Goldberg (ed.), *Conceptual Structure, Discourse and Language*, 113–130. Stanford: Center for the Study of Language and Information.

Fillmore, Charles. 1976. Frame semantics and the nature of language. *Annals of the New York Academy of Sciences: Conference on the Origin and Development of Language and Speech* 280: 20–32.

Fillmore, Charles, Paul Kay, and Mary Catherine O'Connor. 1988. Regularity and idiomaticity in grammatical constructions: The case of let alone. *Language* 64: 501–538.

Fodor, Jerry. 1983. *Modularity of Mind: An Essay on Faculty Psychology*. Cambridge, MA: MIT Press.

Geeraerts, Dirk. 2016. The sociosemiotic commitment. *Cognitive Linguistics* 27(4): 527–542.

Goldberg, Adele. 1995. *Constructions: A Construction Grammar Approach to Argument Structure*. Chicago: University of Chicago Press.

Greenberg, Joseph H. 1963. Some universals of grammar with particular reference to the order of meaningful elements. In J.H. Greenberg (ed.), *Universals of Human Language*, 73–113. Cambridge, MA: MIT Press.

Grice, Paul. 1975. Logic and conversation. In P. Cole and J. Morgan (eds.), *Syntax and Semantics*, volume III: *Speech Acts*, 41–58. New York: Academic Press.

Gumperz, John. 1976. The sociolinguistic significance of conversational code-switching. In J. Cook-Gumperz and J.J. Gumperz (eds.), *Papers on Language and Context, Working Paper 46*, 1–46. Berkeley: Language Behavior Research Laboratory, University of California.

Heath, Jeffrey, Francesca Merlan, and Anne Rumsey (eds.), 1982. *The Languages of Kinship in Aboriginal Australia*, Oceania Linguistic Monograph No 24. Sydney, Australia: University of Sydney Press.

Kegl, Judy, Ann Seghas, and Marie Coppola. 1999. Creation through contact: Sign language emergence and sign language change in Nicaragua. In M. DeGraff (ed.), *Language Creation and Language Change: Creolization, Diachrony, and Development*, 179–238. Cambridge, MA: MIT Press.

Kendon, Adam. 2004. *Gesture: Visible Action as Utterance*. Cambridge, UK: Cambridge University Press.

Lakoff, George. 1982. *Categories and Cognitive Models*. Berkeley: University of California, Institute of Cognitive Studies.

Lakoff, George. 1993. The contemporary theory of metaphor. In A. Ortony (ed.), *Metaphor and Thought*, 202–251. Cambridge, UK: Cambridge University Press.

Langacker, Ronald W. 1987. *Foundations of Cognitive Grammar, Volume 1, Theoretical Prerequisites*. Stanford: Stanford University Press.

Langacker, Ronald W. 1988. A usage-based model. In B. Rudzka-Ostyn (ed.), *Topics in Cognitive Linguistics*, 127–161. Amsterdam: John Benjamins.

Langacker, Ronald W. 1993. Universals of construal. In J.S. Guenther, B.A. Kaiser, and C.S. Zoll (eds.), *Proceedings of the Nineteenth Annual Meeting of the Berkeley Linguistics Society: General Session and Parasession on Semantic Typology and Semantic Universals*, 447–463. Berkeley: Berkeley Linguistics Society.

Li, Thomas Fuyin. 2018. Extending the Talmyan typology: A case study of the macro-event as event integration and grammaticalization in Mandarin. *Cognitive Linguistics* 29(3): 585–621.

Li, Thomas (ed.). 2022. *Handbook of Cognitive Semantics*. Leiden, the Netherlands: Brill.

Michaelis, Laura A. 2001. Exclamative constructions. In M. Haspelmath, E. König, W. Österreicher and W. Raible (eds.), *Language Universals and Language Typology: An International Handbook*, 1038–1050. Berlin: Walter de Gruyter.

Mithun, Marianne. 2007. Grammar, contact, and time. *Journal of Language Contact* 1(1): 144–167.

Peirce, Charles S. 1955. *Philosophical Writings of Peirce*. New York: Dover Publications.

Pustejovsky, James. 1995. *The Generative Lexicon*. Cambridge, MA: MIT Press.

Radden, Günter and Zoltan Kövecses. 2007. Towards a theory of metonymy. In K. Panther and G. Radden (eds.), *Metonymy in Language and Thought*, 17–59. Amsterdam: John Benjamins.

Robinson, Peter and Nick C. Ellis (eds.). 2008. *Handbook of Cognitive Linguistics and Second Language Acquisition*. Mahwah: Lawrence Erlbaum.

Sapir, Edward. 1921. *Language: An Introduction to the Study of Speech*. New York: Harcourt Brace.

Saussure, Ferdinand de. 1959. *Course in General Linguistics*. In E. Bally and A. Sechehaye (eds.) (Translated from the French by Wade Baskin). New York: The Philosophical Society.

Schegloff, Emanuel and Harvey Sacks. 1973. Opening up closings. *Semiotica* 8(4): 289–327. Available at doi:10.1515/se-mi.1973.8.4.289.

Seyfarth, Robert and Dorothy Cheney. 2012. Primate social cognition as a precursor to language. In M.M. Tallerman and K.R. Gibson (eds.), *The Oxford Handbook of Language Evolution*, 59–70. Oxford: Oxford University Press.

Slobin, Dan I. 1996. From "thought and language" to "thinking for speaking." In J.J. Gumperz and S.C. Levinson (eds.), *Rethinking Linguistic Relativity*, 70–96. Cambridge: Cambridge University Press.

Slobin, Dan I. 2006. What makes manner of motion salient? Explorations in linguistic typology, discourse, and cognition. In M. Hickmann and S. Robert (eds.), *Space in Languages: Linguistic Systems and Cognitive Categories*, 59–81. Amsterdam & Philadelphia: John Benjamins.

Talmy, Leonard. 2000a. (T1). *Toward a Cognitive Semantics*, volume I: *Concept Structuring Systems*. i–viii, 1–565. Cambridge, MA: MIT Press.

Talmy, Leonard. 2000b (T2). *Toward a Cognitive Semantics*, volume II: *Typology and Process in Concept Structuring*. i–viii, 1–495. Cambridge, MA: MIT Press.

Talmy, Leonard. 2003. (T3) The representation of spatial structure in spoken and signed language. In B. Hampe (ed.), *Perspectives on Classifier Constructions in Sign Language*, 169–196. Mahwah: Lawrence Erlbaum.

Talmy, Leonard. 2005. (T4) The fundamental system of spatial schemas in language. In B. Hampe (ed.), *From Perception to Meaning: Image Schemas in Cognitive Linguistics*, 199–234. Berlin: Mouton de Gruyter.

Talmy, Leonard. 2007a. (T5) Foreword (Comparing introspection with other methodologies). In M. Gonzalez-Marquez, I. Mittelberg, S. Coulson, and M. Spivey (eds.), *Methods in Cognitive Linguistics: Ithaca*. Amsterdam: John Benjamins.

Talmy, Leonard. 2007b. (T6) Attention phenomena. In D. Geeraerts and H. Cuyckens (eds.), *Oxford Handbook of Cognitive Linguistics*, 264–293. Oxford: Oxford University Press.

Talmy, Leonard. 2011a. (T7) Universals of semantics. In Patrick Hogan (ed.), *Cambridge Encyclopedia of the Language Sciences*, 754–757. Cambridge: Cambridge University Press.

Talmy, Leonard. 2011b (T8). Cognitive semantics: An overview. In C. Maienborn, K. von-Heusinger, and P. Portner (eds.), *Semantics: An International Handbook of Natural Language Meaning*, 622–642. Berlin: Mouton de Gruyter.

Talmy, Leonard. 2015. (T9) Relating language to other cognitive systems: An overview. *Cognitive Semantics* 1(1): 1–44.

Talmy, Leonard. 2016. (T10) Properties of main verbs. *Cognitive Semantics* 2(2): 133–163.

Talmy, Leonard. 2017. (T11) Foreword: Past, present, and future of motion research (Neglected aspects of Motion representation). In I. Ibarretxe-Antuqano (ed.), *Motion and Space across Languages: Theory and Applications*. HCP (Human Cognitive Processing) Series. Amsterdam: John Benjamins.

Talmy, Leonard. 2018a. (T12) *The Targeting System of Language*. Cambridge, MA: MIT Press.

Talmy, Leonard. 2018b. (T13) Combinance in the evolution of language: Overcoming limitations. *Cognitive Semantics* 4(2): 135–183.

Talmy, Leonard. 2020. (T14) Semantic unilocality. *Cognitive Semantics* 6(2): 131–169.

Talmy, Leonard. 2021. (T15). Structure within morphemic meaning. *Cognitive Semantics* 7(2): 155–231.

Talmy, Leonard. 2022. (T16). Foreword: A taxonomy of cognitive semantics. In Thomas Li (ed.), *Handbook of Cognitive Semantics*. Leiden, the Netherlands: Brill.

Talmy, Leonard. 2023. (T17) Relations across cognitive faculties. *Cognitive Semantics* 9(1): 1–17.

Tomasello, Michael. 2010. Cognitive linguistics and first language acquisition. In D. Geeraerts and H. Cuyckens (eds.), *Oxford Handbook of Cognitive Linguistics*, 1092–1112. Oxford: Oxford University Press.

Toratani, Kiyoko. 2024. Open-class-ness, aspect, iconicity, and other characteristics of Japanese ideophones viewed through the lens of closed-class semantics. *Cognitive Semantics* 10(1): 55–83, doi: https://doi.org/10.1163/23526416-bja10059.

Whorf, Benjamin Lee. 1956. *Language, Thought, and Reality*. New York: The Technology Press of Massachusetts Institute of Technology and John Wiley & Sons, Inc.

Wilkins, David P. 1993. Linguistic evidence in support of a holistic approach to traditional ecological knowledge: Linguistic manifestations of the bond between kinship, land, and totemism in Mparntwe Arrernte In N. Williams and G. Baines (eds.), *Traditional Ecological Knowledge: Wisdom for Sustainable Development*, 71–93. Canberra: CRES Publications.

Winer, Gerald A. and Jane E. Cottrell. 1996. Does anything leave the eye when we see? Extramission beliefs of children and adults. *Current Directions in Psychological Science*, 5(5) 137–142.

Young, Robert and William Morgan, with Sally Midgette. 1992. *Analytical Lexicon of Navajo*. Albuquerque: University of New Mexico Press.

Index

adjacency pairs   44
admonitive   24
adverbial pro-clauses   15, 27
Agent   16, 20, 26, 34, 50, 57
anaphor   9, 42, 49, 52, 63
anaphoric trigger   90
arbitrariness   49
associated meaning   30–31, 62
axial properties   15

Baldrick, Chris   65
Beattie, Geoffrey   87
Bernstein, Basil   70
blocked argument   39
Boroditsky, Lera   32
bounded   13, 16, 29, 33, 36, 41, 50
bounding   13, 16
Brennan, Susan E.   41
Brugmann, Claudia   34
bulk encounter   91–92
Bybee, Joan   59

channel   75
channel of communication   75
Cheney, Dorothy   85
chronolects   56
Clark, Eve   38
Clark, Herbert H.   41
classifier   77–79
closed class   6, 28
closed-class morphemes   4, 6, 8, 12, 14–17, 21, 23, 31, 48n7, 51, 61, 65–66, 74, 80, 91
code switching   60
coevent   34, 58, 64, 73
cognitive organizers   80, 82, 84, 86
combinatorial   45, 80
combinatorial structure   84–85, 95
communicative purpose   23, 25, 30, 44, 62, 66
componential analysis   30
conceptual alternativity   38
conceptual category   12–13, 16, 18, 28–29, 38–39, 50, 66–67, 70–71
conceptual representation   89
conceptual structure   1, 8, 55, 60, 93

conformation   83
construals   38
constructive discrepancy   53, 56, 62
content patterning   30, 32, 34
contour   14, 78–79, 92. *See also* intonation contour
core meaning   30–32, 62
core schema   58
Costello, Anne M.   90
Cottrell, Jane E.   84
cue adaptation   54

deictic   9, 20, 35, 42, 47, 54, 58, 66, 76–77, 90
dilation   81–82
direct object   6, 8, 25, 34, 58
direct referent   89

ellipsis   36
Ellis, Nick C.   70
Emmorey, Karen   77
entrenchment   12
event frame   36
evidential   22–23, 81
expressives   71
extramission theory of perception   84

factive representation   89
Fauconnier, Giles   55
fictive chain   76, 88
fictive motion   54, 84
fictive representation   89
Figure   13–15, 24n4, 26, 30, 34, 38, 50–51, 55, 57, 64, 73, 78–79, 83, 91–92
Fillmore, Charles   6n1, 26, 30
Fodor, Jerry   79n11
force dynamics   17, 26, 29, 62, 84
frame semantics   30
framing   40, 42–43, 58, 64

Geeraerts, Dirk   61
Goldberg, Adele   6n1
Greenberg, Joseph H.   72
Grice, Paul   43
Ground   13, 15, 26, 30, 34, 38, 50–51, 55, 58, 64, 73, 78–79, 83, 92

group-level organization   84–85, 95
Gumperz, John   60

hearsay   23
Heath, Jeffrey   91

ideophones   7, 71, 100
implicational universal   72
instrumental   8, 58, 67
intonation contour   5–7, 24, 61
intromission theory of photons   84

Kegl, Judy   70
Kendon, Adam   77
Kövecses, Zoltan   53

Lakoff, George   34, 51, 54
Langacker, Ronald W.   12, 38, 73
language death   70
lexicalizing   12, 30
Li, Thomas   1, 58

macro-event   50, 58
Manner   11, 32–33, 38, 50, 71, 73, 91
methodology   93
Michaelis, Laura A.   25
mimetics   71
mirativity   19
Mithun, Marianne   58
modality   40, 75, 84
modal-request construction   23, 36, 52
mood   25, 75
moot fulfillment   23
Morgan, William   68
motility   13, 16
multiplex   16, 29, 31

n-plural   72

open class   4, 7, 33, 48, 59
open-class morphemes   4, 7–8, 11, 17n2, 31,
   51, 58–61, 66–68, 74, 91, 94
open-class verbs   33
overlapping systems   80, 95

Palpability, Semi-abstract Level of   88
Path   32–34, 58–59, 64, 71, 73
Patient   6, 16, 20, 26, 52
Peirce, Charles S.   49

plexity   16
plural   5, 16, 27, 39, 72, 74, 82, 91
pragmatics   8, 35, 62
pretend addressee   65
privilege of occurrence   73
proverse   34, 51
Pustejovsky James   54

Radden, Günter   53
range of applicability   68
receiver   10, 74–75
repertory   12, 59, 65, 67, 72, 76, 96
restricted code   70
retroverse   51
Robinson, Peter   70

Sacks, Harvey   44
Sapir, Edward   86n12, 91
satellite-framed   32, 58, 64
Saussure, Ferdinand de   48
Schegloff, Emanuel   44
schematic systems   12–13, 25–26, 62, 65–66
sector (of associated meaning)   31–32
semantic bleaching   59
semantic components   12, 14, 16, 27, 30–31,
   47, 52, 62, 65–66
semantic conflict   53–55, 62
semantic unilocality   33
sender   10, 74–75
sensory path   84
sensory qualia   66
Seyfarth Robert   85
signed language   70, 75, 77
Slobin, Dan I.   39, 91
slot (in polysynthesis)   7
somatic-haptic channel   75
somatic-visual channel   75
spatial augments   14
spatial schematization   83
speech-external context   9
speech-internal context   9
state of openness   8
story world   90

Talmy, Leonard   1, 99
targeting   43, 54, 90
targeting gesture   20, 76, 88
thinking for speaking   39
Tomasello, Michael   70

Toratani, Kiyoko   71
trigger   9, 42, 63, 90
turn taking   10, 44, 61
Turner, Mark   55
typology   58, 64, 73, 96

unbounded. *See* bounded
uniplex   16, 29, 31, 48, 54, 74
universality   61

verb-framed   32, 58, 64, 91
versality   33

Whorf, Benjamin Lee   86*n*12, 91
Wilkins, David P.   91
windowing   36
Winer, Gerald A.   84

Young, Robert   68

www.ingramcontent.com/pod-product-compliance
Lightning Source LLC
Chambersburg PA
CBHW021411290426
44108CB00010B/486